America's
Climate Century

America's Climate Century

What Climate Change Means
for America in the 21st Century

and What Americans Can Do about It

by

Senator Rob Hogg

Cover and text layout and design by Mary Ylvisaker Nilsen, Zion Publishing: www.zionpublishing.org.

The back cover photograph, provided by the staff of Iowa Senator Rob Hogg, shows Senator Hogg speaking on the Senate floor in April 2012, thanking Iowa's religious leaders for calling on Iowans of faith to take climate action.

ISBN: 978-1483987156

Copies can be ordered at Amazon.com or Createspace.com. For discounted bulk orders contact the author:

Rob Hogg
2750 Otis Road SE
Cedar Rapids, IA 52403-4708

SenatorRobHogg@gmail.com

Printed in the United States of America
10 9 8 7 6 5 4 3 2 1

For our children,
Robert,
Dorothy,
and Isabel,
and all of your generation
and the generations
that follow

Acknowledgments

Many people helped with this book, and I want to thank some of them publicly for their help. Several climate advocates in Cedar Rapids read early copies of the book, including Renate Bernstein, Charles Crawley, Martin Smith, and Cheryl Valenta. Luther College professor, Jim Martin-Schramm, who serves as president of the board of directors for Iowa Interfaith Power & Light, gave me great feedback about an early draft and shared his experience of writing books. So, too, did Connie Mutel, who also introduced me to Mary Nilsen of Zion Publishing, who assisted with the publication of this book.

I want to thank my former legislative assistant, Laurel Rhame, and my current legislative assistant, Chelsea Krist, for their editorial advice and encouragement.

There are almost certainly mistakes in this book, for which I accept full responsibility, but I know the book is better for everyone's help.

Finally, I want to thank my wife, Kate, our children, Robert, Dorothy, and Isabel, and the rest of my extended family, who read or listened to drafts of this book, for their patience, for the great suggestions they had to make it better, and for the constant reminder of how important this issue is for our future.

Rob Hogg
Iowa State Senator
Cedar Rapids, Iowa
March 2013

Table of Contents

Figures—

Introduction

I began this book in July 2012, when my state, Iowa, like so many other states across our country, was suffering the effects of the worst drought in my lifetime. The drought was the latest climate-related disaster, after so many other climate-related disasters. I wanted to write this book to help Americans understand what climate change means for our country and to get support for the climate action that is so urgently needed for our national self-interests, for today's children and grandchildren, and for future generations.

After I finished a first draft, Hurricane Isaac hit the Gulf Coast, disrupting the Republican National Convention in Tampa and bringing record rainfall to parts of Louisiana. Yet, in his acceptance speech, Governor Romney mocked President Obama for promising to slow the rise of the oceans and to heal the planet, instead of "working for us." It was surreal to listen to a major party candidate use sea level rise as a laugh line while much of Louisiana was under water. I thought climate change was going to become a major issue in the campaign. President Obama fought back, saying that climate change is not a hoax. Then the candidates went silent on the issue. Through 270 minutes of Presidential debates, climate change was not mentioned once.

Then came Hurricane Sandy – an unprecedented storm to hit much of the East Coast in late October with record storm surges through downtown New York City and across New Jersey. It killed Americans, ruined businesses, destroyed homes, and cost our country billions. Mayor Bloomberg endorsed President Obama for re-election because of his position on climate change. Governor Christie set politics aside to work on recovery. Hurricane Sandy reminded millions of Americans that our federal government needs to help state and local governments during disasters.

Hurricane Sandy may come to be seen as the final turning point when Americans demanded climate action. You can help make that happen by advocating for climate action with your elected officials. If you have worked on climate change before and were discouraged by political inaction, you need to renew your efforts now because the political world changed after Hurricane Sandy. Hurricane Sandy gives all elected officials a new opportunity to recognize the need for climate action. It makes clear how high the stakes are. If record storm surges through downtown New York City do not get our attention, what will it take? Are we going to wait until the water is there permanently?

The fight against climate change is so important, and the stakes are so high, that it must become our new national purpose. If current elected officials do not recognize that, we must replace them. Either way, you can help make that happen through your advocacy and, if necessary, by running for office yourself.

I have watched the climate issue closely for more than 25 years since I was an undergraduate student at the University of Iowa. As a graduate student in the early 1990s, I tried to stop the University of Minnesota from rebuilding its coal-burning heating plant. Later, I served as a board member for Minnesotans for an Energy-Efficient Economy promoting state laws for energy efficiency and renewable energy. Before the caucuses in Iowa in 2000, I worked for a faith-based organization, Ecumenical Ministries of Iowa, advocating with presidential candidates in Iowa on a bipartisan basis. Since 2002, I have worked on energy and climate issues as a state legislator representing portions of Cedar Rapids.

As a state legislator, I now realize how difficult it is for elected officials to take action on complicated issues like climate change. In Iowa, we have done some things to address climate change, but not nearly enough to do our part to address the problem. The reason is simple. Elected officials have to deal with thousands of constituents, hundreds of issues, and the constant need to campaign. Very few have the time to understand the climate issue to the extent necessary. And very few have heard from enough citizens in their districts about the issue to take the truly significant action that is so urgently needed. Elected officials across our country must hear from Americans who support climate action.

The fight against climate change must become our new national purpose.

Americans have been patient, too patient, with the climate issue. We did not jump on the first warnings in the 1970s and 1980s. Nor did we rush to action as record high global temperatures were recorded throughout the 1990s and 2000s. After Hurricane Katrina in 2005, we thought long and hard about significant climate action, but then we decided to hold off a little longer.

Despite the delays, I have never lost my hope that we could take effective action. The scientific understanding of climate change has continued to improve. Sustainable technologies have increasingly become the best economic choice, too. Beyond that, I have always had faith that when enough Americans see climate change as a priority, we will be the people who lead the world to confront this challenge. As I first told audiences when I worked for Ecumenical Ministries of Iowa, a "Doubting Thomas" today can become a great leader for climate action tomorrow.

Like Doubting Thomas, Americans have wanted to see the physical evidence that climate change was real before taking action. For me, the event that made climate change a reality occurred in 2008, when the city where I live and which I represent, Cedar Rapids, was hammered by an unprecedented flood. The previous record flood stage on the Cedar River at Cedar Rapids was 21 feet. By June 13, 2008, floodwaters reached their peak at more than 31 feet – more than 10 feet higher than the previous record. The flood forced 25,000 people to evacuate their homes; today, over 1,000 of those homes have been demolished. The flood forced one of our two hospitals to evacuate; that hospital sustained $60 million in damage. The flood forced nearly 1,000 businesses, churches and nonprofits to close at least temporarily, and we lost nearly 200 of them permanently. Eighty percent of the buildings that house city and county government were damaged, including city hall, the courthouse, the main fire station, the police station, the jail, and the library.

Fortunately, no one died in our flood, but every home, every business, and every building that was flooded has a story to tell. For many, the consequences were devastating, both economically and emotionally. Many families lost economic security. As a community, we lost a generation's worth of wealth. The total cost of the flood was calculated at more than $5 billion, or more than $40,000 per resident. (Cedar Rapids is recovering, thanks to billions of dollars of federal and state aid and much charitable help, but our recovery is not yet done.)

I personally believe a flood of that magnitude would not have hit Cedar Rapids without global warming and its resulting climatic changes. We had a wet winter and a wet spring that year and then unprecedented rain in excess of 15 inches over the two weeks leading up to the flood. And it was not just Cedar Rapids. The Flood of 2008 hit dozens of other cities and towns in Iowa, and there were more floods in 2010 and 2011. Since 1990, Iowa has had 15 Presidential disaster declarations due to flooding. These floods provide a "dose of reality" about climate change. It is no longer an abstract issue for me. It is reality.

Because of Hurricane Sandy, climate change is a reality for increasing numbers of Americans. We know we can wait no longer. It is time for climate action.

In this book, I try to provide basic information Americans need to know about climate change in the 21st century and concrete actions you can take that will help fight climate change. Here are the chapters:

- *Chapter 1* provides an overview of the challenge confronting America in "the climate century" – and calls for Americans to take action.

- *Chapter 2* reviews the science of climate change so that you have the knowledge you need to understand what is happening.

- *Chapter 3* details how climate change has momentum that requires us to act long before we know exactly how bad it will be.

- *Chapter 4* summarizes the current and likely future consequences of climate change including ocean acidification, sea level rise, extreme storms, floods, droughts, wildfires, loss of drinking water, infestations of pests, outbreaks of disease, and other biological disruptions.

- *Chapter 5* explains the benefits of moving beyond fossil fuels, not only for climate reasons, but also for national security, public health, job creation, consumer, and economic reasons. Chapter 5 also explains why nuclear is not the answer to climate change.

- *Chapter 6* calls for national climate action by all of us to give ourselves, our children, our grandchildren, and future generations a livable future.

- *Chapter 7* addresses the politics of climate change and the need for Americans to help lead the fight against climate change by advocating with elected officials or by running for office.
- *The Appendix* provides "Responses to Doubting Thomas" to help you when you hear assertions by people who oppose climate action.

You do not need to sit down and read this book straight through, word for word. The headers are a guide for the key words and phrases you can use in your advocacy with elected officials.

In this book, I cite books and reports I have read, as well as news reports that appeared in Iowa or Minnesota. It is not because these sources are the definitive news sources, but they are what I have read and they represent news that has been covered in main street America and that affects main street Americans.

Some people might say I am just preaching to the choir in this book. I disagree. I hope the broader public will read this book. I hope every elected official, every candidate for office, and every political activist will read this book. As I said, even a "Doubting Thomas" can become a leader for climate action.

But this book is also for the choir. Why? Because choir members need encouragement. Choirs need new songs to sing. Choirs need to practice.

Our choir has been given the awesome responsibility of leading America in this climate century, doing the hard work of educating ourselves, of working to inform others, and of taking the climate action that is so urgently needed. This includes the responsibility of leading the world into a new global alliance for sustainability.

Working together, we can do it.

Chapter One
The Climate Century

We are living in the climate century. In this century, every aspect of our lives will be affected by human-caused global warming and its resulting climate changes, and by the actions that are necessary to stop climate change before it devastates our world. Climate change is the defining historical issue of the 21st century.

When I first became involved in the late 1980s, carbon dioxide levels in our atmosphere had just passed 350 parts per million. At that time, the first reports about the effects of global warming on the environment were being written, along with projections of more warming in what seemed like the distant future from the buildup of carbon dioxide and other greenhouse gases in the atmosphere.

In 2013, the situation is much worse. Carbon dioxide levels are now approaching 400 parts per million. The 17 warmest years on record globally have all occurred in the last 18 years. Scientists have measured and assessed other explanations for the warming and have determined that only greenhouse gases from human activities can explain the amount of warming measured to date.

The news is now filled with reports of climate-related disasters: extreme storms, floods, droughts, wildfires, infestations of pests, outbreaks of disease, and other biological disruptions. Already, hundreds of millions of people suffer from climate-related disasters around the world each year. Scientists continue to project, with even more scientific certainty, additional warming over the coming century and escalating damage to our people, our economy, and our natural resources.

Some people say we cannot do anything about climate change because it will hurt our economy. They are wrong. Climate change, if unchecked, will destroy our economy through increasingly frequent and severe climate-related disasters. Climate action, by contrast, will create jobs, save energy costs, and reduce health costs.

Our economy is already feeling the effects of climate change. Climate-related disasters caused more than $50 billion in damage in the United States in 2011. The drought, Hurricane Isaac, and Hurricane Sandy in 2012 cost us much more. At the same time, we continue to import huge amounts of oil, costing us more than $200 billion each year, and the health care costs of coal and other fossil fuels total well over $100 billion each year.

The fight against climate change is urgent not only because of the damage we are already suffering, but also because there is momentum in the warming of the earth that requires us to act long before we know exactly how bad it will be. We are already irreversibly committed to additional warming and climate change. The decisions we make and the actions we take today will determine how much more warming and climate change our children and grandchildren will experience this century. We urgently need to change direction to limit the damage they will experience. Unfortunately, unless we change direction, we are headed for a collision with catastrophe.

This challenge is comparable in magnitude to what my parents' generation experienced in the fight to win World War II and later during the Cold War. Just as my parents' generation did not ask for those conflicts, Americans today did not ask for the challenge of climate change. Once it was forced on them, however, my parents and their generation knew they had to win World War II.

Like them, we must win the fight against climate change now that it has been forced on us. In the same way that Americans were united in the fight against the threat of Communism around the globe during the Cold War, we must be united in the fight against climate change. In this climate century, we must make the fight against climate change our new national purpose.

> What we do now will determine what our children will experience this century.

The good news is that winning the fight against climate change will not require the greatest sacrifices in American history – not even close. But it may require the greatest foresight that Americans have ever had. Americans will need to see ever-growing dangers decades in advance and then unite behind national climate action to prevent as many disasters from happening as possible and to minimize the effects of those that cannot be avoided.

In the climate century, we will not ask our young people to lay down their lives by the thousands in foreign countries. Instead, we will ask ourselves to reduce our energy use through energy efficiency and energy conservation. We will ask ourselves to phase out fossil fuel use in favor of 100% renewable electricity. We will ask ourselves to reject gas-guzzling vehicles and frequent air travel in favor of transportation solutions like fuel efficiency, electric vehicles, rail, teleconferencing, and urban revitalization.

We will also invest in research, development, and deployment of new technology. We will build infrastructure designed to withstand extreme weather. We will invest in our natural resources to give native wildlife and native plants a chance to survive the changing climate. We will support each other to endure the climate disasters of the future that we cannot avoid. Most important, we will lead the world into a new global alliance for sustainability.

Climate policy will take its place at the center of American politics. It is not some "add-on" issue that people can think about after jobs and the economy or taxes and the budget. Climate policy requires knowledge by every elected official, every candidate, and every engaged citizen, regardless of geography or political affiliation. It is the story of our lives. It is the defining historical issue of this generation. If we get this issue wrong, every other issue about which we care will prove to be nothing more than re-arranging the deck chairs on the Titanic.

The stakes are enormous. Based on a relatively stable climate, human population has been able to grow from a few million before recorded history to more than seven billion today. With climate change, the well being of civilization is in grave jeopardy. In this century, the number of people being affected by climate disasters is expected to increase from hundreds of millions annually to billions every year if we do not take urgent action. Climate change is a threat multiplier, too, threatening our national security. Human civilization is ultimately at stake.

The good news is, if we get this issue right, we will not only address the climate problem, we will also address the sources of our recurring economic stagnation. Our investment in new infrastructure, energy efficiency, renewable energy, transportation solutions, and research, development, and deployment of new technology will create millions of jobs in the short run and save consumers billions of dollars in the long run. As we slash our dependence on fossil fuels, we will also slash the costs of imported oil, reduce the health costs of fossil fuels, and usher in a new era with more health, prosperity, and sustainability.

There are many things Americans must do to help in this urgent fight for sustainability and survival. Entrepreneurs, consumers, researchers, workers, and business owners all have a job to do. However, our most important job is the job of citizenship. We must demand comprehensive climate action from Congress and the President, now, and sustain that action for decades to come. We need strong national climate policy and American leadership on a global basis. Those who block climate action by Congress and the President must be held accountable. Elected officials must take climate action, or we will replace them.

Today, young Americans are being born into a world racing toward the brink of climate catastrophe. The momentum is strong. The challenge is enormous. The consequences of our failure would be severe. However, we know that Americans in the past have faced worse, and had to sacrifice more, and have prevailed. We, too, can prevail. Mustering all the hope and courage we can and using all the freedom we possess, we can understand the climate challenge, recognize our new energy and climate reality, and lead our country and the world to take the climate action needed for today and future generations.

By getting involved, you can make a difference. A handful of active citizens in every Congressional district in America can make a difference. Let's grow a movement for the climate action we so urgently need for sustainability, health, and prosperity in the climate century and beyond.

> *Our most important job is the job of citizenship.*

**Senator Rob Hogg's Top Ten List
for Citizen Climate Action**

1. Write, call, and visit your U.S. Congressional representatives and U.S. Senators regularly and ask them to support climate action.
2. Write letters to the editor of your local paper supporting climate action – it helps educate the public, and your elected officials read them.
3. Join or form an organization locally that meets at least monthly dedicated to climate education and advocacy, and publicize its work.
4. Ask another person to write and call your Congressional representatives and Senators to support climate action – then ask another.
5. Share this book through your local library or by loaning it to friends.
6. Reach out to community groups to educate them about climate change and to ask them to support comprehensive climate legislation.
7. Use less energy, less electricity, and less gasoline – and give a portion of the money you save to a climate advocacy group.
8. Buy renewable energy whenever possible, and slash your investments in fossil fuels in favor of investments in sustainability.
9. Manage lands to hold rainwater and to help native wildlife and native plants survive climate change.
10. Support organizations such as the American Red Cross to help with disaster relief and recovery.

Chapter Two
Climate Science

Given the hype about the so-called climate "controversy," I think Americans would be surprised to learn how little is controversial about the science of climate change. There is no controversy about the existence of the natural greenhouse effect, the fact that humans are rapidly adding "greenhouse gases" to the atmosphere, or that these greenhouse gases have a warming influence on the earth. There is also no longer any controversy about the fact that the earth has warmed significantly.

There is now a strong American scientific consensus about climate change. The consensus is that climate change is real, is being caused primarily by human activity, and poses real dangers for our future. This consensus is based on actual climate records, the scientific understanding of the earth's climate history, the physical workings of the climate system, and computer models that are the most sophisticated in the world.

The so-called "controversy" has come from a handful of scientists, interest groups, and political commentators who assert that there is no conclusive evidence that climate change will be catastrophic. They imply that we can continue to burn fossil fuels without limit. That implication is wrong, and their thinking is dangerous. Their views have been rejected by mainstream American science. Even the few scientists who are skeptics acknowledge that greenhouse gases have an influence that is significantly warming the earth.

It is true that there are inherent uncertainties in climate science – after all, this is an unprecedented experiment on the only planet that is our home. This means there is some uncertainty about how much and how fast the earth will warm, and what the local consequences will be. Because of this uncertainty, we need to continue a robust scientific investigation into climate change.

However, the need for more scientific research is no excuse for delay as a policy matter. No skeptic has been able to show that it would be safe for humans to increase greenhouse gases without limit. There are real limits on how many greenhouse gases humans can put into the atmosphere. A number of scientists believe we have already passed those limits. Given the current scientific understanding of climate change, it is not reasonable to delay climate action any longer.

Today's American Scientific Consensus

For many Americans, it is enough that our scientific leaders in this country have come together to reach consensus about climate change. On October 21, 2009, in a letter to the United States Senate, the leaders of 18 professional scientific organizations in the United States stated:

> Observations throughout the world make it clear that climate change is occurring, and rigorous scientific research demonstrates that the greenhouse gases emitted by human activities are the primary driver. These conclusions are based on multiple independent lines of evidence, and contrary assertions are inconsistent with an objective assessment of the vast body of

peer-reviewed science. Moreover, there is strong evidence that ongoing climate change will have broad impacts on society, including the global economy and on the environment. For the United States, climate change impacts include sea level rise for coastal states, greater threats of extreme weather events, and increased risk of regional water scarcity, urban heat waves, western wildfires, and the disturbance of biological systems throughout the country. The severity of climate change impacts is expected to increase substantially in the coming decades.

The organizations that were represented in making this statement are not fringe organizations. They represent the established, mainstream science in the United States in fields such as meteorology, biology, chemistry, geophysics, and agricultural sciences. The leaders who came together to issue this statement included the leaders of the following organizations:

- American Association for the Advancement of Science
- American Chemical Society
- American Geophysical Union
- American Institute of Biological Sciences
- American Meteorological Society
- American Society of Agronomy
- American Society of Plant Biologists
- American Statistical Association
- Association of Ecosystem Research Centers
- Botanical Society of America
- Crop Science Society of America
- Ecological Society of America

- Natural Science Collections Alliance
- Organization of Biological Field Stations
- Society for Industrial and Applied Mathematics
- Society of Systematic Biologists
- Soil Science Society of America
- University Corporation for Atmospheric Research

In 2010 and 2011, the U.S. National Academy of Sciences released a series of reports, *America's Climate Choices*, reflecting the consensus of scientific experts to inform American decision makers about climate change. A 36-page booklet, *Climate Change: Evidence, Impacts, and Choices,* summarizes the state of the knowledge about climate science, providing the evidence that "human activities, especially the burning of fossil fuels, are responsible for much of the warming and related changes being observed around the world." This booklet and the other reports are available to the public at the National Academy of Sciences web site for *America's Climate Choices.*

It is not just national scientific leaders who have concluded that human-caused climate change is real and dangerous for our future. Scientists across the country have reached that conclusion. For example, 138 scientists from 27 colleges and universities in Iowa came together in November 2012 to warn us that "Iowans are living with climate change now and it is costing us money already." They cited "clear statistical evidence" of more extreme precipitation events and deeper droughts under dry conditions. They warned us that "more droughts and floods are likely in the future." These are scientists who teach in our local colleges and universities, who live in our neighborhoods, who have children that attend our schools. They are speaking up because they are concerned about our future.

As late as the 1990s, not every major American scientific organization agreed that we were already experiencing human-caused global warming and its resulting climatic changes. Now they do.

Today, there is no established scientific organization in this country that says the earth is not warming or that greenhouse gases are not a primary cause. They all agree that climate change is happening and is caused primarily by greenhouse gases from human activity.

The Natural Greenhouse Effect

Today's American scientific consensus on climate change did not just emerge overnight in 2009 because of Hurricane Katrina or *The Inconvenient Truth*. Rather, it is the product of decades of thorough scientific research. Nineteenth century scientists, most notably Joseph Fourier of France, first determined that there were gases in the atmosphere that had a warming effect on the earth. In 1896, a Swedish scientist, Svante Arrhenius, calculated that doubling carbon dioxide in the atmosphere would increase global average temperature by 2 to 6 degrees Celsius, or 3.6 to 10.8 degrees Fahrenheit.

Here is how the natural greenhouse effect works. Solar radiation enters the atmosphere and warms up the earth, creating infrared radiation (i.e., heat), some of which radiates back into space. Some of that infrared radiation is absorbed by naturally occurring greenhouse gases. By absorbing heat, these gases keep the planet warmer than it otherwise would be.

Greenhouse gases have the basic property of absorbing infrared radiation in the wavelengths in which it would otherwise radiate into space. Greenhouse gases act like a blanket that traps the heat from a person sleeping at night, or like the glass of a greenhouse that makes it possible to grow plants when it is too cold outside. Without natural greenhouse gases, the earth would be a frozen planet, too cold to support human life, let alone human civilization.

Measured Increases in Greenhouse Gases

Beginning with the Industrial Revolution, humans have been producing so many greenhouse gases that they, over time, have been building up in the atmosphere. I am going to focus on carbon dioxide because it is the greenhouse gas causing the most global warming. Carbon dioxide in the atmosphere is measured in parts per million. Although that measure may sound small, each part per million represents more than two billion tons of carbon dioxide in the earth's atmosphere.

Carbon dioxide does not just wash out of the atmosphere in a few days like water vapor, or even within a few years. Carbon dioxide stays in the atmosphere for more than 100 years, and some other greenhouse gases have an "atmospheric residence" of thousands of years. This means their influence on the climate is irreversible for coming human generations. It is as if we are adding blankets to the atmosphere every year, but when we realize we have too many, we will not be able to kick them off.

Scientists have determined that before the Industrial Revolution, carbon dioxide levels were about 280 parts per million. Continuous measurement of carbon dioxide in the atmosphere began in 1957 at Mauna Loa in Hawaii. Since 1957, the level of carbon dioxide in the atmosphere has increased every year, and the rate of increase is accelerating.

In 2012, the average carbon dioxide level was 393.81 parts per million. Records from ice cores show that this is the highest level of carbon dioxide in the atmosphere in at least 800,000 years. We are rapidly taking carbon that has been stored underground for millions of years in fossil fuels and transferring it into the atmosphere.

Annual average CO_2 levels at Mauna Loa	
Year	CO_2 Level
1960	316.91
1965	320.04
1970	325.68
1975	331.08
1980	338.68
1985	346.04
1990	354.35
1995	360.80
2000	369.52
2005	379.80
2010	389.85

Source: National Oceanic and Atmospheric Administration. Earth System Research Laboratory

The level of carbon dioxide has not only increased every year since measurements began, but the rate of increase is accelerating. In the 1960s, carbon dioxide levels were going up less than one part per million per year. In the 1980s, carbon dioxide levels were going up nearly 1.5 parts per million per year. Since 1995, the increase has been about two parts per million per year. We are adding even more blankets every year than we did in previous years.

Decades of Scientific Research

As early as 1981, the U.S. Council of Environmental Quality prepared the first government report on climate change, entitled "Global Energy Futures and the Carbon Dioxide Problem." At the time, carbon dioxide levels were approximately 338 parts per million.

Sources of Greenhouse Gases

- **Carbon Dioxide** – Carbon dioxide is added to the atmosphere from the burning of coal, oil, and natural gas, and from the permanent destruction of forests.
- **Methane** – Methane is added to the atmosphere from coal mines, pipelines, landfills, flooded land, deforested land, and animal agriculture. It comes from the decay of organic matter in the absence of oxygen.
- **Nitrous Oxide** – Nitrous oxide is added to the atmosphere by certain types of fossil fuel combustion and by the application of nitrogen fertilizers.
- **Water Vapor** – Water vapor is a natural greenhouse gas. Although there is some disagreement, most scientists believe global warming will lead to higher levels of water vapor in the atmosphere because warmer air can hold more water vapor.
- **Other Greenhouse Gases** – Other greenhouse gases come from specific products or industrial processes. Various chlorofluorocarbons (CFCs) and their replacements have been used as coolants and blowing agents. Other greenhouse gases include tetrafluoromethane, trifluoromethane, sulfur hexafluoride, hexafluoromethane, carbon tetrachloride, and methyl chloroform.
- **Not Carbon Monoxide Or Sulfur Dioxide** – Carbon dioxide and other greenhouse gases should not be confused with urban air pollutants like carbon monoxide and sulfur dioxide that create smog or cause acid rain. These pollutants need to be controlled, but they are not greenhouse gases.

In the 1981 report, the Council stated that to limit carbon dioxide to no more than 438 parts per million, global fossil fuel use would need to peak by 2007 (when it was projected that atmospheric carbon dioxide would be 371 parts per million) and then continuously decline over the rest of the 21st century. (In fact, carbon dioxide levels were much higher than that in 2007 – 383.77 parts per million – which means that we now have to reduce our emissions much faster to limit atmospheric carbon dioxide levels to 438 or even 450 parts per million.)

"Global Energy Futures and the Carbon Dioxide Problem" was written at a time when people were concerned about fossil fuel shortages, especially oil shortages. Nonetheless, the Council rejected the argument that we would run out of fossil fuels before climate change would be a problem, stating: "Before global fossil fuel resources can be completely used, CO_2 concentrations (regardless of the assumed rate of increase) will have risen to levels at which, other things being equal, disastrous climate modifications appear inevitable."

The Council calculated that if all fossil fuels were burned, carbon dioxide levels would reach eight to ten times their pre-industrial level, or approximately 2,200 to 2,800 parts per million.

Since 1981, scientific assessments of climate change have repeatedly warned that the earth would warm and that the consequences would be negative, if we did not slow down and stop the buildup of greenhouse gases in the atmosphere. These predictions and warnings were based on a scientific understanding of the earth's climate history, the physical workings of the climate system, and sophisticated computer models. In 1988, for example, the World Conference on the Changing Atmosphere in Toronto warned that "humanity is conducting an unintended, uncontrolled, globally pervasive experiment whose consequences could be second only to a global nuclear war."

In February 1991, in a report entitled *Changing by Degrees*, the U.S. Office of Technology Assessment summarized the science for Congress as follows:

> We appear to be pushing the climate system beyond the limits of natural rates of change experienced by the Earth for hundreds of thousands and probably millions of years. The projected rate of climate change may outpace the ability of natural and human systems to adapt in some areas. While it may be many years before climate monitoring proves global warming is statistically significant, each year that passes increases the severity of the policy actions that would be needed to slow or reverse these climate trends. The IPCC [Intergovernmental Panel on Climate Change] estimates that stabilizing trace gas concentrations at current (perturbed) levels would require an immediate 60 percent reduction in carbon dioxide emissions, 15 percent in methane emissions, and 70 percent in nitrous oxide and CFC emissions.

Later that year, the U.S. National Academy of Sciences issued a report, *Policy Implications of Greenhouse Warming*, detailing mitigation and adaptation measures that could be taken. *The New York Times* summarized the report on April 11, 1991, in a headline: "Quick Action on Global Warming Is Urged by U.S. Science Academy." But very little action was taken. In fact, our greenhouse gas emissions have been increasing.

Warmest Years on Record

Although it was once thought it might be "many years" before human-caused warming could be detected, it is real and is happening now. According to the National Climate Data Center of the National Oceanic and Atmospheric Administration, every year since 1976 has had global average temperatures above the 1901 to 2000 average. The 17 warmest years on record through 2012 have all occurred in the 18 years since 1995.

Warmest Years on Record
Year and temperature difference
(compared to 1901-2000 average)

2010	+0.66°C	2009	+0.59°C	1997	+0.51°C
2005	+0.65°C	2007	+0.59°C	2008	+0.51°C
1998	+0.63°C	2012	+0.58°C	1999	+0.45°C
2003	+0.62°C	2004	+0.58°C	1995	+0.45°C
2002	+0.61°C	2001	+0.55°C	2000	+0.43°C
2006	+0.60°C	2011	+0.53°C		

Source: National Climate Data Center (02/16/13)

I remember headlines in 1995, 1997, and 1998 where scientists reported that the earth's temperature was the "warmest year on record." Not anymore. Those years have been repeatedly passed as the warmest on record.

In October 2011, the Associated Press reported that a prominent skeptic, Richard Muller, a physics professor at the University of California-Berkeley and senior scientist at Lawrence Livermore Laboratories, had completed a comprehensive review of temperature records, and he now agreed that global warming was real.

In 2012, the United States set literally thousands of record high temperatures. In the first six months of 2012, there were nine record high temperatures for every record low in this country. July 2012 was the warmest month ever in American history. Global warming, long predicted, is here.

Decline of Arctic Ice

In the age of the Internet, people can monitor changes in ice cover over the Arctic Ocean almost daily. Satellite measurements go back to 1979. They are currently available at the web site of the National Snow and Ice Data Center in Boulder, Colorado (www.nsidc.org).

In September 2007, ice cover over the Arctic Ocean plummeted to 1.65 million square miles, the lowest level since satellite measurements had begun, more than a million square miles less than the 1979 to 2000 average for September (2.70 million square miles). In September 2011, the ice extent reached the second lowest level on record, just behind September 2007. As the National Snow and Ice Data Center reported at the time, it continued the "decadal trend of rapidly decreasing summer sea ice."

On September 16, 2012, Arctic ice cover plummeted to a new record low of 1.32 million square miles. This was 49% below the 1979 to 2000 average.

Some people say that Americans do not care about the loss of Arctic sea ice. I do not agree with that, but that is not the point. The point is, the loss of Arctic sea ice is another measured reality that shows unequivocally the earth is warming. The earth does not lose more than a million square miles of Arctic sea ice without significant warming and other climatic change.

Not "Just Nature"

Now that experience shows that global warming is real, skeptics are raising a new line of argument: "Isn't that just a coincidence? Isn't it really just nature?" They have tried to convince Americans that warming is being caused by "just nature," not our burning of fossil fuels.

The cause of global warming is not a philosophical

issue about which everyone is entitled to his or her own beliefs. Living in the 21st century, we can resolve the question of causation through scientific measurement and analysis. Global warming may be the most thoroughly studied scientific issue of modern times. The answer: There is no way to explain the amount of warming being experienced without the primary impact of greenhouse gases.

The other proposed possible explanations and influences on global climate – solar variation, urban heat island effect, changes in tropospheric ozone, changes in stratospheric ozone, changes in surface albedo, changes in cloud cover, volcanoes, aerosols, and linear contrails from jets – have all been assessed and measured and do not explain the global warming that is occurring.

Relative Influence on Global Climate
(in watts of heat energy per square meter)

Influence	Warming (Cooling) Effect
Carbon Dioxide	+1.66
Methane	+0.48
Tropospheric ozone	+0.35
CFCs/other halocarbons	+0.34
Nitrous oxide	+0.16
Solar variation	+0.12
Surface albedo (black carbon)	+0.10
Water vapor	+0.07
Linear contrails	+0.01
Stratospheric ozone loss	-0.05
Surface albedo (land use)	-0.20
Sulfate aerosols	-0.40
Cloud albedo	-0.70

Source: Intergovernmental Panel on Climate Change
Working Group I, 2007

As the chart on the prior page shows, greenhouse gases from human activity (carbon dioxide, methane, CFCs and other halocarbons, and nitrous oxide) account for an increase of 2.64 watts of heat energy per square meter. The other measured influences pale by comparison. Greenhouse gases put into the atmosphere by human activity are the primary driver of global warming and climate change.

Not *"A Hoax"*

United States Senator James Inhofe of Oklahoma has repeatedly called global warming "the greatest hoax ever perpetrated on the American people." This is even less true and more damaging to our country than the allegations of Communist infiltration made by Joseph McCarthy during the Red Scare of the early 1950s.

I am not opposed to scientists challenging the mainstream understanding of climate change as a scientific matter. That is a proper part of the scientific process. Hypothetically, if skeptics someday could prove scientifically why global warming is not going to cause any more problems, I would welcome that news. However, I am strongly opposed to the distortion of the issue by some politicians and political commentators who have labeled climate change "junk science" in an effort to confuse the American people and delay the necessary climate action.

I have read and listened to the handful of scientists who are identified as climate skeptics. These skeptics actually confirm much of the climate science, and their disagreements tend to be quite narrow. Listening to Senator Inhofe and political commentators who share his views, the American people would be surprised by how much climate science the skeptics actually confirm.

In a book by climate skeptic Roy Spencer, *Climate Confusion* (2008), he agreed that there is a natural greenhouse effect. He agreed that greenhouse gases are building up in the atmosphere. He agreed that greenhouse gases have a warming influence on the earth. He even conceded that catastrophic warming of ten degrees Fahrenheit might happen. In a second book, *The Great Global Warming Blunder* (2010), endorsed on the front cover by Rush Limbaugh, Spencer

Climate skeptics actually confirm that greenhouse gases are warming the earth.

wrote there is a 50% chance the earth would warm by more than 1.5°C (2.7°F) this century if carbon dioxide levels are allowed to reach 560 parts per million. None of that shows that climate change is "junk science" or "the greatest hoax ever perpetrated on the American people."

I heard another skeptic, Richard Lindzen, speak at the University of Iowa in the late 1990s. He agreed that greenhouse gases have a warming effect on the earth, but he argued that clouds are a self-regulating mechanism that will prevent significant global warming by offsetting most of the warming effect.

As shown in the chart on page 25, however, the IPCC has measured the effects of clouds, and found that they have offset only a small fraction of the warming effect of greenhouse gases to date (-0.70 watts per square meter for clouds compared to +2.64 watts per square meter for greenhouse gases). Again, Lindzen's theory does not show that climate change is "junk science" or "the greatest hoax ever perpetrated on the American people."

As a state legislator, I receive for free in the mail every month a publication by the Heartland Institute called the *Environment and Climate News*. Disseminating such publications is one of the ways skeptic organizations continue to have influence, even as mainstream American science has rejected their views. These organizations also submit guest columns and letters to the editor that appear frequently in small-town newspapers.

In an article in the July 12, 2011 edition, entitled "Spencer-Denning Debate Highlights Heartland Climate Conference," Heartland reported that long-time skeptic Patrick Michaels now calls himself a "lukewarmer":

> Dr. Patrick Michaels, a senior fellow at the Cato Institute and past president of the American Association of State Climatologists, kicked off the conference with a keynote presentation in which he described himself as a "lukewarmer." Humans are influencing global temperatures, Michaels explained, but not enough for temperatures to rise any higher than the lower end of United Nations computer model predictions.
>
> Michaels reported long-term trends indicate approximately 1.4 degrees of warming per century, not enough to produce significant problems.

When a climate skeptic confirms that the earth is warming 1.4 degrees per century (the article did not say whether that was Celsius or Fahrenheit), it defeats the claim that climate science is "junk science" or "the greatest hoax ever perpetrated on the American people." It confirms that greenhouse gases from human activity have a real warming effect and are causing real consequences.

Even if global warming is limited to 1.4 degrees of warming per century, as Michaels claims, it will still raise sea levels. It will still change weather and precipitation patterns. It will still change the ranges of plants, insects, and animals. It will still cause infestations of pests and outbreaks of diseases. It will still cause extreme weather events and climate-related disasters.

In July 2012, a former skeptic, whom I have already mentioned, Richard Muller, wrote an op-ed for the *New York Times* entitled "The Conversion of a Climate-Change

Skeptic," in which he concluded that the world is not only warming, but that humans are almost entirely the cause. In many ways, Muller's conversion represents the end of the climate skeptics.

Even the skeptics agree: In the climate century, the earth will continue getting warmer due to greenhouse gases from human activity.

Chapter Three
Climate Momentum

If there is one concept that has not been explained well to Americans about global warming and climate change, it is the momentum in the warming of the earth that commits us to additional warming even when we decide to stop it.

These factors – thermal lag, warming magnifiers, and the deep cuts in emissions that are required to stop the buildup of greenhouse gases – are key realities that help define the 21st century as the climate century. They also mean that we can approach the brink of climate catastrophe without even knowing it.

Americans, though, are strong enough and smart enough to know that we cannot ignore the warning signs. Americans know that it is our basic creed to make life better for the next generation. Doing so urgently requires climate action.

Thermal Lag

Here is how "thermal lag" or "committed warming" works: Humans are adding greenhouse gases to the atmosphere. In the atmosphere, greenhouse gases exert an immediate warming influence on the earth's temperature, but those gases stay in the atmosphere and continue to exert that warming influence for decades or centuries. Thus, decades or centuries will pass before the full warming from those greenhouse gases is realized.

Yet, we keep adding more greenhouse gases to the atmosphere, even while the earth's temperature is still warming in response to the greenhouse gases we added years ago and decades ago. It is like adding one blanket after another – but when we get too hot, we will not be able to kick the extra blankets off. Instead, we will be committed to getting even hotter due to thermal lag.

When I talk to middle school students about climate change, I tell them it is like cooking macaroni and cheese. When you turn the stove on to boil the water, the water starts warming up, but it does not immediately boil. It takes a few minutes for the heat from the stove to warm the water up to the boiling point.

The same process works for the planet, except that instead of a few minutes, it takes several decades or longer for the earth to reach a new equilibrium temperature based on the warming effect of greenhouse gases. What is worse, unlike the example of macaroni and cheese, we are still turning up the dial on global warming by adding more greenhouse gases to the atmosphere.

In 2007, the Intergovernmental Panel on Climate Change calculated that the "committed warming" from past emissions is at least another degree Fahrenheit over the next six decades. The effect of thermal lag may be even longer. A headline from *National Geographic* on March 17, 2005 said, "Global warming unstoppable for 100 years, study says."

A short wire service news brief with the headline "Irreversible Warming" that appeared on page 7A of the *Cedar Rapids Gazette* on January 30, 2009, reported as follows:

The warming effect humankind has inflicted on the atmosphere will last at least 1,000 years even if the world's smokestacks and tailpipes were to stop spewing greenhouse gases, a new U.S. government report says. NOAA senior scientist Susan Solomon and her team found that even if atmospheric concentrations of carbon dioxide were to decline, the oceans, which have slowed climate change by absorbing heat, will achieve equilibrium with the atmosphere by releasing it back into the air.

Instead of appearing as a news brief on page 7A, "irreversible warming" that will last 1,000 years should be front page news. Not only front page news, but the subject of editorials and essays, of talk shows and news hours.

More importantly, "irreversible warming" should be the topic of political conversation and policy action. In 2007, at a meeting at Roosevelt Middle School in Cedar Rapids, I told then-Senator Obama about my concerns about climate change. He said, "We don't want to leave it for our children to clean up." I told him, "We've already forced our children to clean it up; the question now is whether our children will be able to clean it up." He said, "That's because it's irreversible." He was right.

Warming Magnifiers

Another global warming concept that has not been explained well to Americans is that once started, nature will magnify the warming. Scientists use the label "positive feedback" for forces that will amplify global warming. There is, however, nothing "positive" about them. Like the effect of a magnifying glass, they magnify the warming, so I prefer to use the phrase, "warming magnifiers."

Warming magnifiers include:

- Loss of albedo – the reflectivity of the earth's sur- face – as snow and ice melt, exposing darker water or darker land underneath.
- Loss of vegetation (that otherwise would absorb and hold carbon dioxide) due to pests, disease, wildfire, or other biological disturbance.
- Release of methane (a powerful greenhouse gas) from the permafrost, thaw lakes, and deep oceans in the Arctic region.

Loss of albedo is one of the reasons why the Arctic re- gion is warming faster than other places around the world. It is also why black carbon has a warming effect as soot darkens snow and ice around the world.

In 2011, there was record heat and drought in Tex- as. Reports later in the year estimated that the heat and drought killed 500 million trees in Texas. When large numbers of trees die, it turns a carbon sink into a carbon source. If the trees are burned in a brush pile or a wildfire, the carbon dioxide they absorbed is released immediately back to the atmosphere. If they decay naturally, the carbon is released back to the atmosphere over years. The loss of the 500 million trees in Texas increased that state's already heavy greenhouse gas emissions by several percent, magni- fying global warming.

Something similar is happening in Colorado as the pine bark beetle kills the forests of the Rocky Mountains. Something similar is happening in the Midwest as invasive species, like the emerald ash borer and gypsy moth, kill our trees.

The magnifying effect of methane is potentially the most serious. Methane is now being released in the Arctic region as the permafrost thaws, and as melting ice forms new thaw lakes. Methane is a potent greenhouse gas, twenty times more powerful than carbon dioxide per molecule, and large releases of methane from the permafrost, thaw lakes, or deep oceans could be catastrophic.

Warming magnifiers create the danger that, once set in motion, human-caused global warming will trigger runaway global warming. The risk of runaway global warming from warming magnifiers makes the fight against climate change that much more urgent.

Deep Cuts in Emissions

Climate change poses another challenge that has not been adequately explained to the American people, namely, that stopping the buildup of greenhouse gas emissions in the atmosphere will require deep cuts in emissions. Deep cuts are required because carbon dioxide and other greenhouse gases stay in the atmosphere for decades if not centuries.

As stated before, the U.S. Office of Technology Assessment reported in 1991 that stopping the buildup of greenhouse gas concentrations in the atmosphere would require "an immediate 60 percent reduction in carbon dioxide emissions, 15 percent in methane emissions, and 70 percent in nitrous oxide and CFC emissions."

Of those requirements, only the cuts in CFC emissions have been made, thanks to President Reagan who signed the Montreal Protocol in 1987 and the first President Bush who strengthened that protocol in 1991 to phase out CFCs globally. The Montreal Protocol had as its primary purpose the prevention of further stratospheric ozone depletion, and it has worked. Reagan and Bush listened to the scientists, worked with interested parties, and engaged in diplomacy to deal with the global environmental threat of ozone depletion.

As for the other greenhouse gases, emissions of carbon dioxide, methane, and nitrous oxide have all increased since 1991. That means the required cuts to stop further increases in atmospheric concentrations are now even deeper than were required before.

Unfortunately, there is no simple technological fix for this problem. Unlike sulfur dioxide emissions, which have been reduced through technological innovation and the regulations of the Clean Air Act, there is no feasible device that can be put on a smokestack to remove emissions of carbon dioxide or other greenhouse gases.

Some have proposed technology to capture carbon dioxide from the smokestacks of fossil fuel burning plants and bury it in underground reservoirs. So far, these proposals for "carbon capture and sequestration" (CCS) are neither feasible nor cost-effective. CCS technology requires so much energy that power companies would need to build additional power plants simply to operate the equipment. CCS proposals would require construction of an enormous network of pipelines to transport captured carbon dioxide to areas with geological formations believed to be suitable for long-term carbon storage.

> Deep cuts in carbon pollution are required because carbon dioxide stays in the atmosphere for decades.

In a proceeding before the Iowa Utilities Board in 2007, carbon sequestration was assessed for a proposed coal plant that was to be built "CCS ready." Ultimately, the coal plant proposal was dropped, but the study showed that the cost just to transport the carbon dioxide from Iowa to Kansas for deep storage was $18.75 per ton, or more than $100 million each year for the expected production of carbon dioxide from the single coal-burning power plant.

CCS is not a cost-effective way to reduce greenhouse gases compared to energy efficiency and renewable energy. The additional power plants and the cost of carbon pipelines would raise the cost of coal-fired power far above that of wind, biomass, biogas, solar, and other renewable energy alternatives. It would be cheaper, cleaner, and quicker to give every American solar panels and energy-efficient refrigerators than to build coal plants with CCS technology.

Moreover, there are no proven examples of long-term, large-scale underground carbon storage. There are a few examples of underground carbon storage, but nothing on the magnitude that would provide reservoirs for every coal plant in America or around the world. Underground carbon storage runs the risk of leaks that would put the carbon dioxide in the atmosphere anyway.

Because there is no technological fix to put on a smokestack, the deep cuts in greenhouse gas emissions will require a different approach. We need to leave fossil fuels in the ground and replace them with fuel-efficiency, energy efficiency, and renewable energy. The deep cuts that are required make the fight against climate change that much more urgent.

Dangerous Climate Change

The forces that create climate momentum are taking us quickly toward dangerous climate change. As I have watched America's political leaders scurry about trying to deal with their self-imposed "fiscal cliffs," it has occurred to me that we are approaching the brink of a "climate cliff" that would be much more catastrophic and should be a much higher priority for our political leaders.

Since the United Nations Framework Convention on Climate Change, signed by President Bush and ratified by the U.S. Senate in 1992, America and the other nations of the world have recognized the need to prevent "dangerous anthropogenic interference" with the climate system.

While many of America's political leaders have ignored this issue and hoped it would go away, scientists and international negotiators have tried to define "dangerous" climate change. Negotiators have said two degrees Celsius, or 3.6 degrees Fahrenheit global average temperature increase, is dangerous. Scientists have said even lower levels of warming are dangerous. In the meantime, people across our country and around the world are already living with the consequences of a "safe" level of climate change.

Global warming has already warmed the earth more than 1.5 degrees Fahrenheit, and due to thermal lag, the earth is irreversibly committed to another degree Fahrenheit warming. We are running out of time. It will require an urgent, all-out effort to avoid "dangerous anthropogenic interference" with the climate system.

On May 30, 2007, NASA's Goddard Institute for Space Studies reported on scientists' efforts to define "dangerous anthropogenic interference" as follows:

> Based on climate model studies and the history of the Earth the authors conclude that additional global warming of about 1°C (1.8°F) or more, above global average temperature in 2000, is likely to be dangerous.... According to study co-author Makiko Sato of Columbia's Earth Institute, "the temperature limit implies that CO_2 exceeding 450 [parts per million] is almost surely dangerous, and the ceiling may be even lower."

To repeat, 450 parts per million of carbon dioxide is "almost surely dangerous," and "the ceiling may be even lower." A number of scientists now believe that 350 parts per million is the only "safe" level of greenhouse gases in the atmosphere – a level that motivates the work of the advocacy group, 350.org.

We already passed 350 parts per million more than 20 years ago, and we are now less than a generation away from 450 parts per million.

In 2008, I was a speaker for a conference of the National Caucus of Environmental Legislators in Chicago, where I was also visiting my sister and her family. As I was preparing my remarks, I asked my then 9-year-old niece to help me with a math problem. I told her that carbon dioxide levels were 386 parts per million, and were increasing at a rate of two parts per million per year. I asked her, at that rate, how long would it take for carbon dioxide levels to pass 450 parts per million? Her answer, "That's easy, Uncle Rob, it would be 32 years." I realized that in 32 years, she would be 41 years old – my age at the time.

It is time for Americans to take climate action for the next generation of Americans. We cannot wait until the crisis is upon us.

In the familiar story of *The Titanic*, the captain was told to disregard the hazards and sail faster because, it was believed, the ocean liner was indestructible. When the look-outs spotted the iceberg ahead of the ship, it was too late. The ship had so much momentum that the captain could not take evasive action.

Like an ocean liner, global warming has momentum, due to thermal lag, warming magnifiers, and the deep cuts in emissions required to stop the buildup of greenhouse gases in the atmosphere.

Because of that momentum, we will not be able to stop global warming immediately, even when we decide to stop it.

Because of that momentum, we do not have the luxury of waiting to see exactly how bad it will be before we take action.

We see danger ahead of us. We urgently need to slow down and change directions before we collide with catastrophe.

Chapter Four
Climate Consequences

What does global warming and climate change actually mean for America? On a cold day in January, a little global warming does not sound so bad. However, the reality is that global warming and climate change are already causing serious negative consequences for America, consequences that will grow increasingly more severe in the coming decades.

This century, climate consequences include:

- sea level rise
- extreme storm events
- flooding and drought
- loss of drinking water
- loss of native species
- infestations of pests
- outbreaks of disease
- heat waves
- wildfires.

Around the world, these changes threaten to disrupt or destabilize societies, leading to new dangers for America. Americans will necessarily face some of these consequences because of the irreversible momentum in global warming. The challenge is to limit future climate change to something manageable. That means we need to slash greenhouse gas emissions to limit future warming and climate change, at the same time that we must protect ourselves and our property from the climatic changes that can no longer be avoided.

Ocean Acidification

There are serious negative consequences from the buildup of carbon dioxide in the atmosphere even without considering global warming. As reported by *National Geographic* in "The Acid Sea" in April 2011, about 30% of the carbon dioxide produced from human activities over the last 200 years has been absorbed in the oceans. While that has slowed down global warming, the carbon dioxide absorbed in the oceans forms more carbonic acid, acidifying the oceans. Every hour, the world's oceans are absorbing more than a million tons of carbon dioxide, more than 8 billion tons every year.

Since the Industrial Revolution, the earth's oceans have already become 30% more acidic. By 2100, unless humans significantly reduce the amount of carbon dioxide emissions from fossil fuel use, the oceans are expected to absorb so much carbon dioxide that they will be 150% more acidic than they were in 1800. Ocean acidification is irreversible by humans - one of the many reasons we need to slash carbon dioxide emissions as soon as possible.

Ocean acidification is already affecting the relative composition of species in the oceans. The rate and amount of acidification is so tremendous, however, that more drastic declines in ocean life are possible. News reports in 2012 said that oceans are now acidifying faster than at any time in the last 300 million years. Our emissions of carbon dioxide are directly endangering coral reefs and ocean life independent of any warming effect carbon dioxide has. This threatens food supplies and biodiversity that America and the world need in the 21st century.

The buildup of carbon dioxide in the atmosphere is also affecting the composition of species on land. As I first learned reading *Climate Change and the Global Harvest,* a 1998 book by Cynthia Rosenzweig and Daniel Hillel, higher carbon dioxide levels favor some plants over others. It now appears, for example, that plants like poison ivy and woody vines thrive under higher concentrations of carbon dioxide, which helps them out-compete other species. Similarly, higher carbon dioxide levels favor some insects over other insects and animals. This could hurt human health, agriculture, and biodiversity around the world.

Higher carbon dioxide levels also reduce the work required of plants to take in carbon dioxide, which in turn reduces transpiration (or evapotranspiration) by plants. Less transpiration by plants can affect local weather conditions and unique ecosystems like rain forests that depend on transpiration by plants. Increased carbon dioxide is a direct threat to rain forests, biodiversity, and natural ecosystems, on top of the other threats already confronting them.

The fact that carbon dioxide levels are rising, and rising faster, is undisputed. That means we are in for a number of dangerous environmental changes, regardless of the global warming effects of carbon dioxide.

Sea Level Rise

Global warming has even more serious consequences for America and the world. Sea level rise is perhaps the most tangible and potentially devastating consequence of global warming. It may not directly affect places like Iowa, but it will hurt Americans and disrupt our economy.

During the last Ice Age, when so much water was contained in the vast ice sheets that covered North America, ocean levels were significantly lower than today. This allowed ancient people to cross the land bridge now under the Bering Strait from Asia to North America, and had other real consequences for people.

As the Ice Age ended, ocean levels rose nearly 400 feet. For the last 6,000 years, ocean levels have been relatively stable. As Iowa native James Hansen explained in his 2009 book, *Storms of My Grandchildren,* it is one of the reasons there is a human civilization. Stable ocean levels allowed people to settle along oceans, live close to their abundant resources, accumulate wealth during lifetimes and across generations, and build modern human civilization.

Today, all of that is threatened by sea level rise.

Global warming causes ocean levels to rise in two ways. First, the level of the ocean rises because of thermal expansion of the water. As water warms, it expands, causing ocean levels to rise. This is a gradual increase in ocean level. So far, it has been measured that ocean waters at the surface are about one degree Fahrenheit warmer than they were in the Nineteenth Century. Ocean levels have risen almost one foot over that time.

The second way that global warming causes ocean levels to rise is that, as land-based ice melts, more water runs off into the oceans and raises sea level. The melting of land-based ice will raise sea levels much faster, and much higher, than thermal expansion by itself.

Sea level rise will not just be a gradual process. In some places, the effects of sea level rise will be sudden as storm surges consume areas and pull them into the ocean. Storms like Hurricane Katrina and Hurricane Sandy actually pulled many acres of land into the sea.

In the United States, the Atlantic Coast is in grave jeopardy because sea level rise caused by global warming is combining with land subsidence. Even small increases in sea level would jeopardize hundreds of thousands of acres of low-lying lands in states like North Carolina.

The Nature Conservancy is working to slow down the effect of sea level rise in the Alligator River National Wildlife Refuge off the coast of North Carolina. By marking where the coast was several years ago, and where it is now, the effect of sea level rise has been made visible. Efforts to rebuild reef barriers, restore wetlands, and plant native trees can slow down the effects of sea level rise and help stabilize the coast.

Rising seas and storm surges threaten to displace millions of Americans this century.

According to research by Benjamin Strauss of Climate Center, released March 13, 2012, more than one percent of America's population (3.7 million people) would be displaced by the now-expected sea level rise of 3.3 feet by 2100. Sea level rise of that amount would put large parts of Louisiana, Florida, and the states bordering the Chesapeake Bay under water.

Globally, sea level rise threatens hundreds of millions of people, entire countries, and generations' worth of wealth. A 3.3-foot sea level rise would displace 17 million people in Bangladesh alone. In turn, that would create new humanitarian and foreign policy challenges for America.

Although the most likely scenario for sea level rise by 2100 is now 3.3 feet, scientists are warning that sea level could rise as much as seven feet this century. Remember, whatever rise in sea level occurs by 2100, it will continue to rise for decades into the 22nd century because of the momentum in the climate system. We need to act now to slow down sea level rise in the climate century and beyond.

In July 2012, Greenland experienced record melting – 97% of the ice cover was melting for several days during that month. If all of the ice covering Greenland eventually melts, sea levels would rise globally by 20 feet. If all of the ice in the world melted, it would raise sea levels by more than 200 feet.

According to James Hansen, when the world was last three degrees Celsius (5.4° Fahrenheit) warmer than today, about three million years ago, the land where the City of Boston is now located was under 80 feet of water. A three-degree Celsius warming of the earth is likely, especially if we do not slash greenhouse gas emissions soon.

Melting Glaciers

In addition to raising ocean levels, the loss of land-based ice will also hurt water supplies in America and around the world.

For America, the loss of glaciers and snow melt in the West threatens water supplies on the Colorado and the Columbia Rivers and also rivers fed by snow melt from the Sierra Nevada. At the same time, rising temperatures are expected to increase the demand for water along those rivers. This combination of reduced water supply and increased demand threatens agriculture, electrical production, and drinking water in California, Colorado, and throughout the West.

The same threat exists around the world, especially in South America and Asia. As global warming melts glaciers and reduces snow pack, large populations will be put at risk. For America, these global impacts will create significant economic, humanitarian, diplomatic, and security issues.

Weather and Precipitation Changes

The melting of ice due to global warming is clear. The fact that global warming has an impact on weather events like floods and drought is just as clear, but it is not as simple to explain. That is why scientists use the term "climate change."

Global warming does not mean it will be just a little bit warmer everywhere every day. Rather, it means that weather and precipitation patterns will change. It means unusual weather that is extreme compared to historical experience. As the earth continues to warm, weather and precipitation will keep changing. It will be significantly warmer in some places at some times; other places may be colder; but overall, more places will be warmer than what used to be regarded as normal. Because of ongoing climate change, there will be no "new normal" in its place.

Here is another way to think about it: The earth has warmed more than a degree Fahrenheit on average since 1900. That means there are already more than 365 additional degree-days of heat Fahrenheit under our blanket of greenhouse gases over the course of a year.

That extra heat might mean that the weather is a little bit warmer every day in some places, or it might mean several weeks a year that are more than 15 degrees higher than the past average. It might mean that some places have similar temperatures to what they had in the past, while other places – like the Arctic – are rapidly warming.

With climate momentum, we will soon see even more heat distributed around the planet. Two degrees Fahrenheit warming means an additional 730 degree-days over the course of a year. Three degrees Fahrenheit means an additional 1,095 degree-days over the course of a year. Additional warming means even more heat distributed around the world.

In a stable climate, as time passes, there should be fewer and fewer temperature records. In the first year records were kept, every reading was a record high and a record low. In later years, there would be fewer records. Yet, after 150 years of records in places like Iowa, we are setting more records, not fewer.

For every record low there were two or three record highs, until 2012, when the record highs out-numbered the record lows by many times. The risk of deadly heat waves, like what Chicago experienced in 1995, what Europe experienced in 2003, and what Russia experienced in 2010, is growing.

The increase in overall heat is bound to change precipitation, too. In 1990, the Intergovernmental Panel on Climate Change identified this problem as follows: "An important hydrological consequence of global warming is potential changes in runoff extremes, both high and low. . . . Thus, attention must be focused on changes in the frequency and magnitude of floods and droughts in evaluating societal ramifications of water resource changes."

Eight years later, in their book, *Climate Change and the Global Harvest*, Cynthia Rosenzweig and Daniel Hillel wrote that climate change "is quite likely to change the hydrological regimes of entire regions."

That is what we have been experiencing. In 1993, the Midwest suffered massive flooding. In 1997, there was massive flooding along the Red River in Minnesota and North Dakota.

On April 29, 1997, the *Minneapolis Star-Tribune* quoted John Firor, then senior scientist at the National Center for Atmospheric Research, as follows: "A warmer earth means that more water evaporates from oceans and rivers, and it means the air can hold more water . . . which means the creation of more powerful weather systems that release more water from the atmosphere in the form of unusually heavy storms."

On May 4, 1999, the *Des Moines Register* ran a headline, "State faces more floods, study warns." This increased risk of flooding was primarily due to an expected increase in winter precipitation, meaning more snow and ice, greatly increasing the probability of events like the Flood of 1993, according to Tom Wigley of the National Center for Atmospheric Research in Boulder, Colorado. As predicted, Iowa has experienced more floods.

Contrary to the skeptics, just because we have extreme snowfalls does not mean that global warming is a hoax. When there is an unprecedented snow or ice event, global warming may very well be a contributing factor, because of changes in weather and precipitation patterns.

> More floods and more droughts, long predicted, are already happening.

In fact, due to global warming and climate change, more extreme winter precipitation events are expected.

In the same way, when drought hits, it will be worse. Warmer temperatures cause more evaporation, making the drought even drier. This is what happened in Iowa and across the nation in 2012.

As Rosenzweig and Hillel explained, these changes mean that the past is less reliable as a predictor of the future. In the climate century, we will see the effects of our greenhouse gas experiment with the planet. Unfortunately, we do not know exactly what the consequences will be in particular locations.

For example, should Iowans – farmers, engineers, those in business or city government – count on more rain than normal, or should we expect drier conditions? Iowa is located between the drier conditions of the Great Plains and the wetter conditions of the Great Lakes. Which way will global warming and climate change take Iowa or any other location in the world? It is hard to know in any given year. What we do know is that the weather in Iowa will not be like it was in the past.

Geological records and computer models can help Americans determine how climate change is likely to affect our cities, our watersheds, our states, and our regions. But we have to pull our heads out of the sand, pursue the knowledge that we need to anticipate climate change, and be prepared for more frequent severe weather and precipitation events in the climate century.

America's Falling Great Lakes

Unlike the effect of climate change on the oceans, climate change is not expected to raise the levels of inland lakes like the Great Lakes. In November 2012, I saw a presentation by Paul Roebber, a professor of freshwater sciences at the University of Wisconsin in Milwaukee, who explained that reduced ice cover over Lake Michigan due to winter warming has led to longer evaporation seasons. Lake levels have been falling since the mid-1990s, even though precipitation levels had not decreased. The Drought of 2012 significantly accelerated this problem.

In early 2013, the U.S. Army Corps of Engineers reported that water levels in Lake Michigan and Lake Huron hit a record low, and were also falling in the other Great Lakes. The Corps reported that this was due to increased evaporation and the Drought of 2012.

With more warming and longer evaporation seasons, lake levels are expected to fall even lower in the future. Falling Great Lakes water levels will have significant adverse economic consequences for shipping, recreation, and waterfront landowners, and will also cause severe damage to lake-front ecosystems.

Ranges of Plants, Insects, and Animals

Global warming will warm the earth and change weather and precipitation patterns. Those changes in weather and precipitation – in addition to the direct effects of higher carbon dioxide – will in turn change the ranges of every plant, every insect, and every animal.

These changes are already well underway. On August 19, 2011, the *Christian Science Monitor* reported on a study of more than 1,300 species over 40 years, which found that, on average, the species had moved toward higher latitudes at a rate of eleven miles per decade. In January 2012, the U.S. Department of Agriculture issued a map with revised vegetation zones moving north to advise gardeners and landowners on what species they should plant.

For more than 20 years, scientists have warned that climate change jeopardizes species such as polar bears and the Monarch butterfly. On February 25, 1992, the *Minneapolis Star Tribune* ran an article headlined, "Ruin of Many Species Feared if Global Warming Proceeds." Already, species are endangered by habitat loss and poaching; climate change is making that threat even more serious.

In 2012, Ducks Unlimited stated on its web site that it had examined "the best available science" and concluded that "climate change poses a significant threat to North America's waterfowl that could undermine achievements gained through more than 70 years of conservation work." Ducks Unlimited and partner organizations like Trout Unlimited, Pheasants Forever, the Izaak Walton League of America, the Wildlife Management Institute, and the Theodore Roosevelt Conservation Partnership have issued two reports, *Seasons' End* (2008) and *Beyond Seasons' End* (2010), that explain the risks to hunting and fishing from climate change, and propose strategies to protect wildlife from its consequences.

In 1998, in *Climate Change and the Global Harvest,* Rosenzweig and Hillel concluded that "agricultural pests, overall, are likely to thrive under conditions of increasing atmospheric CO_2 and rapid climate change." Today, mosquitoes are thriving as the climate changes, causing severe harm to human health. Pine bark beetles of the Rocky Mountains are thriving due to warmer winter temperatures, causing severe harm to the forests and the economy of the region.

Changes in heat, precipitation, plants, and pests are a formula for more frequent and severe wildfires. Unusually wet years bring more growth. Unusually dry and hot years bring more severe drought. Changes in weather and precipitation bring pests and diseases that kill plants. More dead vegetation, under dry conditions, is a tinderbox for more frequent and severe wildfires.

Natural ecosystems have intricate relationships that are now in danger. If a plant cannot pollinate at the right time, the plant species will decline. If a generation of a species is born before or after its food has arrived, that generation will fail. If a predator, a competitor, or a pest is pushed into new territory and destroys native species, there will be little if anything people can do about it.

> Climate change is already affecting agriculture, forestry, and daily activities like gardening, hunting and fishing.

Across America, people are already fighting invasive species. Global warming and its resulting climatic changes are making that problem much worse and much harder to fight.

Climate change will also undermine the resilience of natural ecosystems. It is hurting species that otherwise would be important to climate adaptation. Loss of native species, loss of habitat, new invasive species, more infestations of pests, and more outbreaks of disease will make our effort to combat climate change much harder. The sooner we start the fight, the better our chances.

Climate Disasters

In May 2011, I wrote a guest column for the *Des Moines Register* entitled, "Era of Climate Disasters Has Begun." That column was submitted as flood waters rolled down the Lower Mississippi River, when the dikes protecting southeast Missouri were blown up to spare the town of Cairo, Illinois, and the town of Millington, Tennessee was inundated. While the column was pending publication, a deadly tornado tore through Joplin, Missouri.

In that column, I reviewed recent climate disasters that had affected Iowa, the United States, and the world. Those disasters included the Floods of 2008 that struck Iowa so hard. In 2010, Iowa had flooded again.

Around the country disasters included:

- record drought and wildfires in Texas
- record wildfires in California and Colorado
- deadly tornadoes throughout the South
- record flooding in Tennessee and Rhode Island
- record drought in Georgia
- the unprecedented infestation of Rocky Mountain forests by the pine bark beetle.

Globally, there were even more severe disasters:

- record flooding in Pakistan in 2010 that killed 5,000 and displaced 13 million
- record heat in Russia in 2010 that killed 50,000
- record flooding in Brazil and Australia in early 2011.

Since I wrote that column in May 2011, there have been even more climate disasters. The United States set the record for the warmest twelve-month period in history. The resulting disasters include:

- Record heat and drought that again ravaged Texas and Oklahoma
- Record wildfires in Arizona, New Mexico, Texas, Colorado, Oklahoma, and Montana
- Enormous rains in Montana that triggered flooding down the entire Missouri River valley including western Iowa
- Record floods that hammered Minot, North Dakota, and Dubuque, Iowa
- Hurricane Irene and Tropical Storm Lee that

brought record floods to Vermont and Pennsylvania, respectively.

Overall, in 2011, the United States set a record with 14 billion-dollar disasters at a total cost over $52 billion dollars – more than $165 per American.

In 2012, there were more climate disasters, including nation-wide drought, record flooding in Duluth, Minnesota, record rains from Tropical Storm Debby in northern Florida, and record rains from Hurricane Isaac in parts of Louisiana.

Then came Hurricane Sandy.

With record storm surges through downtown New York City and across New Jersey and other East Coast states, Hurricane Sandy killed more than 100 Americans, ruined businesses, destroyed homes, disrupted public services, ruined public infrastructure, and cost our country billions. By the end of 2012, the total damage from Hurricane Sandy alone had grown to more than $70 billion – well over $200 per American.

We have had so many disasters in recent years that it is hard to remember earlier disasters like Hurricane Ike (2008), Hurricane Wilma (2005), and Hurricane Rita (2005). Even Hurricane Katrina (2005) has become a distant memory. Serial climate disasters are, unfortunately, a reality of the climate century.

In September 2009, I was attending a meeting of the National Caucus of Environmental Legislators in Minneapolis, where I met Senator Debbie Dawkins of Pass Christian, Mississippi. One morning during the conference, *USA Today* had a story headlined "Many in Mississippi still lack homes after '05 storms." I showed the article to Senator Dawkins. She knew the homeless man featured in the article who had been a homeowner before Katrina.

As anyone who has survived a climate disaster knows, climate disasters have real consequences for real people: lost homes, lost wealth, lost possessions, lost productivity, injuries, trauma, and even death.

Americans are not just affected by climate disasters in our own country. In 2011, massive flooding in Southeast Asia disrupted our economy. The drought throughout Australia in 2005 and 2006 caused large increases in global food prices. The Russian heat wave in 2010 did the same, contributing to uprisings in Egypt and other countries in North Africa and the Middle East.

These disasters have enormous humanitarian consequences, too. Killer storms such as Cyclone Nargis in Burma (2008), Typhoon Ketsana in the Philippines (2009), Typhoon Morakot in Taiwan (2009), and Tropical Storm Washi in the Philippines (2011) all call out for a humanitarian and diplomatic response. In 2011, Taiwan asked the Iowa Senate for a resolution supporting its request to join the United Nations Framework Convention on Climate Change, in part because of the devastation from Typhoon Morakot in 2009.

I know that disasters like these have happened throughout human history, occasionally with larger death tolls because societies were less prepared to deal with them. Human mismanagement in the past has contributed to disasters like the Dust Bowl and the Mississippi River flood of 1927. Even without climate change, we should be prepared for disasters like these in the future. Climate change makes the need to prepare that much more urgent.

I recently heard climate change compared to steroid use by baseball players. Players have always hit home runs without steroids, but with steroids, they can hit more of them. It is not possible to say which home run was caused by steroids, but steroids increased the number of home runs. Likewise, climate change is contributing to more frequent and severe climate disasters today.

In 1999, the Red Cross stated, "Climate change is no longer a doomsday prophecy, it's a reality. Changing climate means changing disaster patterns." In 2009, the Red

Cross stated, "The average number of people affected by climate-related natural disasters annually has reached an estimated 243 million." Climate disasters are a reality in the climate century.

Threat Multiplier

Global warming and climate change are pushing sea levels higher, causing heat waves, floods, and droughts, endangering water supplies, contributing to infestations of pests and outbreaks of disease, and bringing more frequent and severe climate disasters. Dealing with these consequences is hard enough, but in a world already filled with problems – war, violence, religious and racial strife, famine, poverty – dealing with them will be much, much harder.

In April 2007, the Military Advisory Board of CNA issued a landmark report, *National Security and the Threat of Climate Change*, in which it labeled climate change a "threat multiplier" for instability in already volatile regions of the world. Its conclusion: "Projected climate change poses a serious threat to America's national security."

As nations experience more climate disasters they will search for the resources necessary to manage these disasters and to meet the immediate needs of their people for food, fresh water and energy. This will surely create additional conflicts between countries.

The residents of nations affected by climate change will all too often become environmental refugees searching for shelter, food and security.

> Unfortunately, serial climate disasters are a reality of the climate century.

Such refugees are created by disasters within countries also. In Cedar Rapids, we still have people living here who first came from the Gulf Coast to flee the damage of Hurricane Katrina.

I know people who left Cedar Rapids following the Flood of 2008, including one former constituent who moved to New Jersey, only to lose her home again from Hurricane Sandy. We need to help our fellow Americans who are victimized by climate disasters. Beyond that, will Americans also be willing to welcome millions from around the world who are fleeing the effects of climate change in their homelands?

The Climate Century By 2080

On March 11, 2007, the *Cedar Rapids Gazette* ran a front page Associated Press article headlined, "Report to Predict Droughts, Floods." It was based on the proceedings where scientists were assembling a report on climate impacts for the Intergovernmental Panel on Climate Change.

The article explained that what is currently happening due to climate change "is nothing compared to the future." Here was the article's summary of "likely results" from global warming:

- "Hundreds of millions of Africans and tens of millions of Latin Americans who now have water will be short of it in less than 20 years. By 2050, more than 1 billion people in Asia could face water shortages. By 2080, water shortages could threaten 1.1 billion to 3.2 billion people."
- "By 2080, between 200 million and 600 million people could be hungry because of global warming's effects."
- "About 100 million people each year could be flooded by 2080 by rising seas."

These numbers are staggering. Water shortages will come from worsening drought and the loss of water supplies when glaciers have totally melted. Hunger will come from additional crop failure due to flood, drought, heat, and pestilence. Floods will come from extreme precipitation events, storm surges, and rising seas.

These "likely results" are not that far in the future. Although 2080 sounds far off, we all know people who will be alive in 2080. They are our children and our grandchildren. Children born in 2012 will just be getting ready to retire in 2080. If we care about their future, we need to care about this issue.

The article finished with good news. Many of the projected effects from climate change "can be prevented . . . if within a generation the world slows down its emissions of carbon dioxide" and "if the level of greenhouse gases . . . in the atmosphere stabilizes."

That is the challenge of the climate century.

Chapter Five
Beyond Fossil Fuels

The fight against climate change requires a new attitude about fossil fuels, coal, oil, and natural gas. The current thinking, which is to develop as much coal, oil, and natural gas as soon as possible ("drill, baby, drill") needs to be replaced by a new understanding: "leave them in the ground."

Scientists have calculated that if we want to limit global warming to no more than two degrees Celsius, or 3.6 degrees Fahrenheit, we need to limit future carbon dioxide emissions to approximately 500 billion tons between now and 2050, or about 13 billion tons per year, with even lower levels of emissions after that. If that is the acceptable limit of warming, then that is our maximum global carbon budget. If that is actually more warming than we can safely handle, then our global carbon budget is even less than that.

We Americans currently produce 6 billion tons of carbon dioxide a year by ourselves. Globally, the people of the world are currently producing more than 30 billion tons of carbon dioxide each year. Unless we dramatically cut our fossil fuel emissions, we would blow by the 500 billion ton limit in less than 20 years. There is no time to waste in moving beyond fossil fuels. That is why we need to leave fossil fuels in the ground.

The good news is that by moving beyond fossil fuels, we can also create jobs, grow businesses, improve public health, and provide clean air and clean water. The current fossil fuel economy is not working for our health, our economy, or the environment. In short, moving beyond fossil fuels is necessary for climate reasons. It will also work for our economy, our health, and our country.

Era of High-Cost Oil

In the climate century, fossil fuels are more expensive and more environmentally destructive than ever before. High-cost oil is part of the new energy reality that is shaping the climate century.

From an economic standpoint, the basic problem is that cheap, readily accessible fossil fuels have been depleted, and we are now going to more extremes for more expensive, more environmentally damaging fossil fuels.

American oil production peaked in 1970. This was not unexpected. American leaders warned our trading partners at the time that we could no longer be the reservoir of oil for the free world.

According to the U.S. Energy Information Administration, oil production peaked in the United States in 1970 at 3.5 billion barrels of oil. By 1980, oil production had fallen to 3.1 billion barrels. In the 1980s, President Reagan encouraged a "drain America first" strategy to defeat the Soviet Union economically. Because the Soviet Union was an oil exporter, we could hurt the Soviet economy by increasing our own oil production to help drive down the price globally. So we increased our oil production to nearly 3.3 billion barrels by 1985 – part of President Reagan's successful strategy to win the Cold War.

However, the "drain America first" strategy also meant that American oil production would later fall more rapidly than it otherwise would have. By 1990, U.S. oil production had fallen to less than 2.7 billion barrels. By 2004, oil production fell below two billion barrels. In 2008, U.S. oil production was just over 1.8 billion barrels, 48% less than production in 1970, and 45% less than production in 1985. Although oil production has since been increased, it is still below oil production levels in 1970 or 1985.

At the same time, oil imports into the United States have soared. In 1970, when the United States was producing 3.5 billion barrels, we imported less than 0.5 billion barrels into our country. In other words, we were producing more than 85% of the oil we consumed.

By 1975, despite the OPEC oil embargo of 1973, oil imports had grown to 1.5 billion barrels. The "drain America first" strategy helped reduce oil imports to less than 1.2 billion barrels by 1985, but after that, oil imports increased rapidly. In 1986, oil imports passed 1.5 billion barrels again. In 1989, oil imports passed two billion barrels. In 1994, oil imports passed 2.5 billion barrels, and then passed three billion barrels just three years later. Oil imports in the United States peaked in 2006 at nearly 3.7 billion barrels. By that time, the United States was producing just one-third of the oil we consumed.

The damaging consequences of our rapidly growing dependence on foreign oil were not just based on the amount of oil imported, but also its cost. In 1997, when the United States first imported more than 3 billion barrels of oil, each barrel cost less than $20, for a total impact of less than $60 billion a year. The drain on our economy was under $200 per American – costly, but manageable.

Then oil prices began their dramatic climb. On August 28, 2001, the *Cedar Rapids Gazette* front page headline declared, "Gas Prices May Hit Record." At the time, gas prices had hit $1.66 per gallon. Oil prices had risen that summer to hit $27 per barrel.

In June, 2004, the cover of *National Geographic* announced "The End of Cheap Oil." By that time, oil prices had risen above $35 per barrel.

In 2005, after Hurricane Katrina, gas prices in Iowa

topped $3 per gallon for the first time. By 2008, the price of a barrel of oil first passed $100 per barrel. On June 13, 2008, gas prices hit $3.85 per gallon – a price frozen in time when the Flood of 2008 inundated gas stations and their owners went out of business.

Oil prices from 1998 to 2008 (June of each year)	
Year	**Price**
1998	$13.72
1999	$17.92
2000	$31.82
2001	$27.60
2002	$25.52
2003	$30.66
2004	$38.03
2005	$56.35
2006	$70.95
2007	$67.49
2008	$133.88

Source: U.S. Energy Information
Administration

At the higher price (more than $100 per barrel) and at higher levels of oil imports (more than three billion barrels per year), Americans were shipping more than $300 billion a year out of this country for foreign oil, leading our country into the Great Recession. Higher oil prices meant less money for other purchases, which lead to more defaults on home loans and the near collapse of America's financial system. Although the price of oil dropped with the Great

Recession in 2008, it never fell as low as its 2004 levels, and has been consistently above $70 per barrel since October 2009. The era of cheap oil is, indeed, over.

If there is a single reason the American economy remains sluggish, it is that we are spending nearly $300 billion a year more for virtually the same amount of oil we imported in the late 1990s. If we had that additional $300 billion to spend in our own domestic economy, rather than paying for foreign oil, we could provide wages and benefits worth $60,000 a year to five million Americans. The high cost of foreign oil, and our dependence on it, is a killer for our economy.

We need to wean ourselves from fossil fuels and learn to leave them in the ground for climate reasons. The high cost of fossil fuels should push us to do so for economic reasons as well.

National Insecurity

As we move beyond fossil fuels, we will also benefit from reduced dependence on foreign oil and the military costs associated with guarding the international trade in oil.

The top 15 countries from which we Americans import oil include Saudi Arabia, Venezuela, Nigeria, Iraq, Colombia, Angola, Kuwait, Russia, and Algeria. With oil prices between $70 and $110 per barrel, we are shipping nearly $100 million dollars to Saudi Arabia every day, nearly $35 billion every year.

In addition to funding foreign countries, we are also spending billions for our military related to defending the international trade in oil. Depending on the study, these costs range at the low end from a few billion a year to more than $200 billion per year, according to a 2010 study by Roger Stern, an economic geographer.

By reducing our dependence on foreign oil and other

fossil fuels, we can slash the costs of oil imports and reduce the costs of our military spending around the world.

Fossil Fuels and Health

Fossil fuels take an enormous toll on the health of Americans. A 2009 study by the U.S. National Academy of Sciences estimated that fossil fuels cause the premature deaths of nearly 20,000 Americans each year and impose $120 billion in health costs on Americans annually, or nearly $400 for each American. Other researchers, such as Paul Epstein at Harvard Medical School, put the health costs of coal by itself at more than $175 billion a year – or more than $560 per American. By any measure, the health care costs caused by pollution from coal and other fossil fuels are enormous.

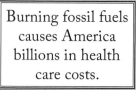

Burning fossil fuels causes America billions in health care costs.

Fossil fuel burning pollutes the air with particulates, sulfur dioxide, nitrogen oxides, carbon monoxide, and heavy metals like mercury. In turn, these pollutants cause or contribute to bronchitis, asthma, other respiratory diseases, heart disease, and neurological disorders. When people suffer these problems, they and their families not only incur substantial health care costs, they also lose economic productivity during the time they must devote to medical care and treatment.

The fuel cycle of fossil fuels also produces health problems. The hazards of coal mining, oil drilling, natural gas production, coal transportation, and disposal of coal ash all add to the health care costs of our country.

By slashing the use of coal and other fossil fuels in order to slash greenhouse gas emissions, we can also significantly reduce health care costs in America.

Extreme Energy

The exhaustion of cheap, readily accessible fossil fuels means we are producing more expensive, more environmentally damaging fossil fuels. I first heard the phrase "extreme energy" from Jeremy Symons of the National Wildlife Federation. It means that every type of fossil fuel being produced today is the product of extreme energy production techniques that are more costly economically and more environmentally dangerous than previous techniques.

Extreme energy includes mountaintop removal coal mining, hydraulic fracturing ("fracking") for oil and gas, deep-water oil drilling, and the development of the tar sands of Canada.

Oil drilling in the deep oceans is much more costly than producing oil in the middle of Oklahoma or Texas was in the 1960s and 1970s, and it is even more damaging to the environment. The Deepwater Horizon explosion in May 2010 killed 11 workers, injured 17 others, and led to the worst oil spill in American history – even worse than the Exxon Valdez in 1989.

Yet, in 2012, the Obama Administration approved the first deep-water oil drilling in the Arctic Ocean. Understanding climate change, that makes absolutely no sense. It also creates grave danger to the environment in the Arctic. Fighting an oil spill in the American Gulf Coast for several months was hard enough; fighting that same type of spill in the Arctic Ocean would be virtually impossible.

Extreme energy includes the development of the tar sands of Canada. Oil from the tar sands is very costly and energy-intensive to produce. It produces 10 to 40% more greenhouse gases than conventional oil per gallon of gasoline.

The production of oil from the tar sands is ruining the boreal forests of Canada. It is turning the boreal forests from a carbon sink into a carbon source. Producing tar sands is polluting wetlands and other natural areas essential for waterfowl. It is destroying lands important to the First Nations of Canada.

The proposed Keystone XL pipeline would endanger the Sand Hills of Nebraska and the Great Plains with oil spills. A tar sands pipeline has already caused a major oil spill on the Kalamazoo River in Michigan. The Keystone XL pipeline would endanger other rivers and water supplies, including water for the Oglala Lakota Nation.

The Keystone XL pipeline also jeopardizes other American values. It would allow a foreign corporation to condemn American farms and ranches for the construction of a pipeline to transport foreign oil to Port Arthur, Texas, for sale on the global market. That is why I call the project the Keystone "Export" pipeline.

Again, understanding climate change, none of this makes any sense. We need to stop the destruction of our environment for the production of fossil fuels that we cannot burn for climate reasons.

Nuclear and Climate

With all the problems with fossil fuels, some people have suggested that the answer to climate change is nuclear power. The nuclear industry promotes itself heavily as "carbon free" power. That is not true, but what is even worse, the nuclear industry's publicity campaign about "carbon free" energy has caused significant delays in climate action. The presence of nuclear power "as an option" has convinced some political leaders that if climate change turns out to be as bad as predicted, we can always "go nuclear."

That thinking is badly flawed. Most obviously, nuclear poses its own significant risks, including the risk of catastrophic accidents (like Chernobyl and Fukushima) and the risk associated with very long-term radioactive waste management. We do not have, and are not going to have, a long-term radioactive waste depository any time in the near future. Even if Yucca Mountain were usable, it would not be able to accommodate the quantity of the high-level nuclear waste that has already been generated in this country. We should not trade the risks of climate change for the risks of nuclear power.

But that is only the simplest argument against nuclear. A deeper understanding shows that the whole concept of a "nuclear option" is flawed.

Nuclear currently produces about 8% of the total energy used in the country with 104 nuclear power plants. If America decided to undertake a significant expansion of nuclear to try to combat climate change, it would require us to construct 1,000 new nuclear plants at a cost of more than $10 billion per plant – an investment of more than $10 trillion. (If we made a similar investment in energy efficiency and renewable energy, we would slash greenhouse gas emissions without the risks associated with nuclear.)

Currently, America imports 90% of the uranium it uses in its existing fleet. Some observers believe we have already reached peak uranium production globally. In other words, we could not sustain a significant long-term expansion of nuclear with current uranium supplies. A major expansion of nuclear would make us even more dependent on imported uranium.

Moreover, the nuclear fuel cycle already involves some of the most fossil fuel intensive industries in the world. It is not "carbon free." Uranium mining, uranium enrichment, uranium mine remediation, and long-term radioactive waste management all require significant use of fossil fuels. As high-grade ores of uranium are depleted, it takes even more fossil fuel energy to produce the same amount of uranium.

> Nuclear is not "carbon free" because it involves fossil-fuel intensive uranium industries.

In her 2006 book, *Nuclear Power Is Not the Answer,* Dr. Helen Caldicott suggested that as high-grade ores of uranium are depleted, the carbon footprint of nuclear energy would become as large as that of natural gas. Given the need for radioactive waste management over the very long-term and the need for fossil fuels to help manage radioactive waste, we make a very long-term commitment to fossil fuels if we build new nuclear power plants.

Nuclear advocates say, however, that we can always reprocess nuclear waste. That approach is also highly dangerous and badly flawed. Reprocessing nuclear waste has enormous financial costs and poses grave dangers to the workers involved. Nuclear waste reprocessing necessarily produces weapons-usable nuclear materials, which makes the fight against nuclear weapons proliferation much more difficult than it already is. At the end of the day, reprocessing nuclear waste still leaves significant high-level radioactive waste. Nuclear waste reprocessing is a dead-end street.

As the climate changes, nuclear becomes even more problematic. There have been numerous reports of nuclear plants being closed because of extreme weather and climate disasters. Across the river from Iowa, the Fort Calhoun nuclear plant had to remain closed because of flooding on the Missouri River in 2011. Other plants worldwide have had to close because of drought and lack of water supply to cool their reactors. With more frequent and severe climate disasters in the future, nuclear is even more risky than before.

Americans already have the challenge of managing the nuclear waste and other nuclear materials that have already been produced. We already have the challenge of stopping nuclear weapons proliferation, which, unfortunately, has already failed in India, Pakistan, and North Korea. India used its civilian nuclear power program to develop nuclear weapons. A major expansion of nuclear would make our current challenges that much harder.

In the climate century, nuclear is not the answer.

Climate and Sustainability

Climate change is the defining challenge facing human civilization this century, but it is not the only threat to sustainability. As suggested above, we face numerous other threats to our future: environmental damage, resource depletion, economic stagnation, rain forest destruction, loss of biodiversity, habitat loss, species extinction, invasive species, ocean pollution, land pollution, air pollution, nuclear waste, nuclear risks, and nuclear proliferation.

All of these problems are linked, and climate change exacerbates all of them. In the climate century, political leaders need to understand all of these problems because we cannot simply trade one problem for another. We need to find common solutions for all of the threats to sustainability in the climate century.

One common solution: moving beyond fossil fuels and leaving them in the ground. For climate safety, for our economy, for our health, for clean air and clean water, and for global security, we need energy efficiency, fuel efficiency, and 100% homegrown renewable electricity – as soon as possible.

Chapter Six
National Climate Action

For thirty years, Americans have debated whether to prevent global warming through emission reductions or try to adapt to climate changes as they happen. The truth is, we have used the debate as an excuse to do nothing. The reality is, we now urgently need to do both.

On October 21, 2009, the leaders of 18 American professional scientific organizations outlined the required course of action in a letter to the United States Senate:

> If we are to avoid the most severe impacts of climate change, emissions of greenhouse gases must be dramatically reduced. In addition, adaptation will be necessary to address those impacts that are already unavoidable. Adaptation efforts include improved infrastructure design, more sustainable management of water and other natural resources, modified agricultural practices, and improved emergency responses to storms, floods, fires and heat waves.

Now – after the heat and drought of 2012, after Hurricane Sandy, after all of the recent climate disasters – we know these actions are even more urgent.

Like Americans before us who had to deal with global crises such as World War II and the Cold War, we have to deal with climate change. Some Americans have resisted climate action for fear it would require us to give up "our way of life." But the changes we need to make do not require the greatest sacrifices in our history, not even close.

We do need to make changes. We need to leave fossil fuels in the ground by using less energy, less electricity, and less gasoline. We need more energy efficiency and energy conservation. We need 100% renewable electricity. We need transportation solutions like fuel-efficient cars, electric vehicles, rail, and main street and downtown revitalization. We also need more staycations and teleconferencing instead of air travel, and more walkable, bike-able, and transit-friendly communities. We need more investment in infrastructure to withstand extreme weather events. We need to protect and enhance our natural resources so native wildlife and native plants can survive climate change. We need more Americans to choose to live simply, so that others may simply live. But a life of drudgery is not required.

What is required is for Americans to demand that our political leaders take national climate action. The fight against climate change must become our new national purpose. We must tell our elected officials and candidates that we support policies, and we are willing to make changes in our lives, to fight climate change and achieve sustainability. The good news is, while slashing our greenhouse gas emissions, we can build stronger, safer, healthier, more vibrant, and more prosperous communities – now and for future generations.

Lifestyle Changes and Policy Advocacy

A growing number of people believe that the key to fighting global warming is individual lifestyle change. If enough people change their lifestyles to reduce their own fossil fuel use, it might bring about a broad social movement for conservation that would help slash greenhouse gas emissions in this country and around the world. Imagine the whole country working together in order to change our lives to reduce emissions, improve health, and build stronger and safer communities. Imagine the whole world trying to imitate our new American conservation ethic.

However, by themselves, lifestyle changes are not enough. Because climate change is driven by global emissions of greenhouse gases, we need national policies and international alliances to combat climate change. Because we live in an era of climate disasters, we need to re-direct society's resources toward disaster prevention, disaster relief, and disaster recovery.

To do that, we need national climate action. We cannot effectively limit climate change and mitigate future climate disasters without national policy. In order to change policies, we need climate education, advocacy, and leadership. We need leaders for climate action who educate the public, advocate with elected officials at all levels, and even run for office to make climate action happen.

Here is a personal example to show why public policy is so important.

I am 46 years old, and currently drive about 25,000 miles per year, using about 500 gallons of gasoline a year in my hybrid. I drive a lot because of my job as an Iowa state senator, because of my climate advocacy, because I am the parent of three active children, and because I gave up air travel for climate reasons in 2002. I could choose to never drive again in an effort to fight global warming. Assuming my current rate of consumption over the next 40 years, that would avoid 20,000 gallons of gasoline, or about 250 tons of carbon dioxide emissions. (Each gallon of gasoline produces 20 pounds of carbon dioxide directly, along with another 5 pounds or more through the gasoline fuel cycle, for a total of 25 pounds of carbon dioxide per gallon.)

Here is the problem: Not driving for 40 years would be equivalent to shutting down a single coal-burning power plant for only 26 minutes! That would help a little, and I am more than willing to reduce my driving to help fight climate change, but obviously it is not enough by itself to get the job done. We need citizens to educate, advocate, and lead for climate action that replaces large coal plants with energy efficiency and 100% homegrown renewable electricity.

Part of your advocacy can include telling your elected officials about your lifestyle changes to reduce your carbon footprint and telling them you are willing to do more to support policies to fight climate change. By telling them, elected officials would know that there was growing grassroots support for climate action. In other words, lifestyle change can support public policy to fight climate change.

Lifestyle change to reduce fossil fuel energy also provides one other advantage: moral authority. Former Vice President Al Gore has been repeatedly crit-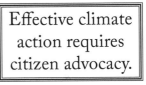

Effective climate action requires citizen advocacy.

icized because he flies too much and uses too much energy at his "home" in Tennessee. While unfair - Gore runs a significant business operation out of his home - it is yet another excuse for inaction to which we need to respond.

We have no more time for excuses. We need American leaders who are committed both personally and politically to the fight against climate change.

In this fight, we need effective public policy to reduce greenhouse gases and mitigate disasters in order to limit climate change to something that will be manageable. These policies must be sustained for decades. That means we need concerned citizens, candidates, and elected officials to engage in education and advocacy. We need citizens who are willing to make changes in their lives so that elected officials understand they can implement the policies we need.

We need today's political leaders and future leaders – in other words, we need you – to understand climate change and to make the fight against it our new national purpose.

Less Energy, Less Electricity, Less Gasoline

The easiest way to reduce emissions of greenhouse gases is simply to use less energy through energy conservation, energy efficiency, and fuel efficiency. We need public policy at the national level to encourage energy savings and to help American families and businesses implement energy savings. I want to share some personal stories in order to reassure you that you do not need to give up your "way of life" in order to save energy, but if you want to change your life to reduce energy use, that's not a bad thing.

According to the Energy Information Administration, the average household electricity consumption in 2010 nationally was 958 kilowatt-hours per month. Look at your electrical bills to see how many kilowatt-hours you use each month, and see if you can reduce your electrical use and save money. Over the past decade, Americans all over the country have worked to reduce their carbon footprint, finding that they not only helped fight climate change, but they also helped themselves by lowering gas and electric bills. This is what my family has been able to do with little sacrifice but by paying attention to energy use in our lives.

At our home, my family of five tries to keep our electrical bills under 500 kilowatt-hours (kWh) a month. In 2011, our monthly electrical use ranged from a low of 281 kWh in October to a high of 592 kWh in July. Our average was 419 kWh per month – or less than half of the national average of 958 kilowatt-hours per month. In July, when we peaked at 592 kWh, we only used 116 kWh during on-peak hours and 476 kWh during off-peak hours, under our time-of-day pricing plan, helping reduce our costs and reducing the demand for peak electricity.

When we moved into our house in 1999, our windows needed replacing, so we installed Energy Star windows. We bought an energy-efficient Energy Star refrigerator. We use other Energy Star appliances including our clothes washer and our dryer. We use energy-efficient compact fluorescent light bulbs, and are starting to use LED lights.

We try to turn off our computer, appliances, lights, and other electrical equipment when not using them. We are reducing our "plug load" by unplugging phone chargers and other unused electrical equipment. I tell my kids that we need to save the electricity to not only fight climate change, but also to ensure that others will have enough electricity for their needs.

We do use the air conditioner in the summer and the natural gas furnace in the winter, but we have them tuned up annually. We turn the temperature up during the day and down at night to reduce energy costs and reduce greenhouse gases. I take short showers – Navy showers my Dad used to call them – using less hot water, especially in the summer months.

Many activities we can do in our lives use little or no fossil fuel energy. Reading a book by yourself or to your kids or grandkids. Encouraging your kids to play outside with the neighbors. Going for a walk in the neighborhood. Even writing your Congressional representative about climate change. We all need to develop a conservation ethic that asks us, "How can I conserve energy today? What simple activities can I do that require little or no energy use? What big decisions can I make about my home and car, my vacations and travels that will reduce my energy use?"

What you do at home you can also do at work. We need business owners and employees to work together to cut energy use in every workplace in America. Businesses can invest in energy efficiency, and employees can help reduce energy use. In fact this is already happening. Many businesses are cutting their energy use through energy efficiency investments and better energy management, often paying off the costs of their investments in a matter of months or just a few years.

Architects led by Ed Mazria have adopted the 2030 Challenge, through which every new building in America by 2030 will be carbon neutral, by cutting their energy use and meeting their energy needs through renewable energy.

Public policy can help us cut our energy use:

- by requiring every utility to implement cost-effective energy-efficiency programs such as refrigerator recycling and incentives for energy-efficient appliances and insulation.
- by continuing to raise energy efficiency standards for lighting and appliances.
- by requiring every public building to be a green building, and providing incentives for construction companies to build green buildings and to renovate existing buildings to make them green.
- by creating training programs for builders and workers to build energy-efficient buildings.

As for gasoline consumption, the average American driver uses 1.49 gallons of gasoline a day, or 10.44 gallons a week, or 544 gallons of gasoline a year, according to the National Association of Convenience Stores. Some drivers use much more than this. Look at your gasoline consumption, try to drive less, and make sure the next vehicle you buy gets at least 40 miles per gallon.

In our family, we have made buying fuel-efficient cars a priority in our family budget. My most recent fuel-efficient hybrid cost about $28,000, including all of the fees and taxes that come with car purchases, which is less costly than many other vehicles on the market. I tell my family and friends that my hybrid is my luxury car. It is the quietest, most elegant vehicle I have ever driven, and I average over 50 miles per gallon.

One of the things I like to do to save energy is to bike to work, which allows my wife or my teenagers to drive the hybrid for their activities. When I am biking, I bike carefully, to avoid accidents – accidents have a very high carbon footprint – and I often think to myself, "Take that global warming!" or "Take that Exxon Mobil!" or "Take that OPEC!" By using less energy, we not only cut emissions from fossil fuels, we also deprive energy companies of some of the money they have used in the past to block national climate action. Every time you buy gas, you pay for some of those negative campaign advertisements that attack clean energy solutions.

When we travel, we travel by car. As I mentioned, I gave up air travel in 2002 for climate reasons. Air travel is the most fossil fuel intensive form of travel, even when calculated on a per passenger basis. You may not need to give up all air travel in the climate century, but you do need to reduce your air travel to a minimum.

This is the difference it makes. In 2011, when we went to visit my Dad who retired to the Denver area, the five of us got in our hybrid, and we were in Denver 15 hours later (including breaks). Round trip, we used about 40 gallons of gasoline at a cost of about $140, producing about 1,000 pounds of carbon dioxide. If we had flown, our share of the round trip to Denver would have been well over 3,500 pounds, at a significantly higher financial cost, and we would still have needed to rent or borrow a car to drive around Denver.

Overall, I drive about 25,000 miles each year, burning around 500 gallons of gasoline. If I drove the same distance with a car that got only 30 miles per gallon, I would burn an additional 330 gallons of gasoline a year at an additional cost of more than $1,000, and produce an extra four tons of carbon dioxide each year. If my car got only 20 miles per gallon, I would burn an additional 750 gallons, pay an additional $2,400, and produce 10 tons of extra carbon dioxide.

Here is the point: Fuel efficiency works. Energy efficiency works. Energy conservation works.

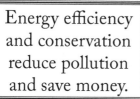

Energy efficiency and conservation reduce pollution and save money.

They all reduce fossil fuel use, reduce emissions, and save money. They do not mean you have to give up the comforts of modern life.

Public policy should support fuel efficiency, energy efficiency, and energy conservation. We need to increase fuel efficiency standards, which the Obama Administration is doing with plans to raise the standard to 54.5 miles per gallon by 2025. We need more incentives for consumers to buy fuel-efficient vehicles.

We could also lower the speed limit back to 60 or even 55 miles per hour. Driving 55 instead of 75 can improve your gas mileage about 20%. (I know there are people who won't like that proposal, but lowering the speed limit would be a small sacrifice to reduce our dependence on foreign oil, save money, and cut our greenhouse gas emissions. If you don't like it, that's fine – that's true for every proposal I make in this book – but then you need to support more of something else that helps us fight climate change.)

Above all, we need comprehensive national climate policy to put an increasing price on carbon pollution so that all consumers have an incentive for more fuel-efficiency, more energy efficiency, and more energy conservation.

Saving energy is not hard. Saving energy does not require us to spend money like millionaires or to live in a monastery. Every American can help save energy. The important thing is to start doing one thing, and then another, and always let your elected officials know you support policies that reduce energy use through fuel efficiency, energy efficiency, and energy conservation.

100% Renewable Electricity

After fuel efficiency, energy efficiency, and energy conservation, the next strategy for reducing fossil fuel use and greenhouse gas emissions is to use 100% renewable electricity. The fight against global warming and climate change is so urgent we should aim for 100% renewable electricity no later than 2030.

At our home, we already have 100% renewable electricity through our local utility's program called Second Nature. I would rather have national policy to move us toward 100% renewable electricity, but I am still glad that our utility offers the Second Nature program. It is a way, at least symbolically and financially, we can support 100% renewable electricity. If and when you sign up for green power through your local utility, please be sure to let your elected officials know that you have done that and that you support public policies to promote renewable electricity.

In Iowa, we produce 20% of our electricity from wind power, the leading percentage in the country. Unfortunately, one of the secrets is that Iowa utilities sell their green power credits to other states to help them meet their higher renewable electricity standards. We need to do even more with wind power in Iowa, and we need to diversify our renewable electric sources to do more with solar power, biomass, biogas, and hydro retrofits on existing dams.

Critics say that renewable electricity is intermittent and not economic. That is misleading at best.

Hydro retrofits on existing dams can provide continuous power. Biomass and biogas generation are dispatchable, just like coal and natural gas. If we build enough biomass and biogas generators, then renewable electricity is as reliable as a system based on coal and natural gas.

Moreover, wind and solar are much more reliable than critics suggest. Solar power achieves maximum production during summer days when electrical use peaks in most states. New wind technology is increasingly effective at lower wind speeds, raising the percentage of time that wind is producing electricity. Wind power is also more reliable if generation sites are spread around a region and are connected by modern transmission lines. To the extent that wind and solar remain intermittent, we can match these sources of electricity with better "demand response" programs that pay large customers to save electricity.

As for the economics of renewable electricity, new wind is already cheaper than new coal or new nuclear. New biomass and biogas systems are cost competitive with new coal and cheaper than new nuclear. Solar energy continues to fall rapidly in price as economies of scale are achieved.

In 2007, the largest solar photovoltaic array in Iowa was seven kilowatts at a nonprofit eco-spirituality center called Prairiewoods. In 2012, Luther College in Decorah installed a system that is 40 times larger – 280 kilowatts. Putting any significant cost on coal to account for its carbon pollution and its health effects would make wind, solar, and biomass clear economic winners.

If we get serious about solar power, we could generate electricity from rooftops of homes and businesses, solar gardens, industrial sites, and other urban areas and roadsides throughout the country.

If we get serious about wind power, we could continue to build wind farms throughout the Midwest and Great Plains and provide the transmission systems needed to get wind power to the urban centers of the east coast.

If we get serious about biomass, we could pay farmers to plant trees and prairie grasses on marginal lands, which will sequester carbon dioxide in the short run and provide a source for sustainable biomass in the long run. Such investments would also provide watershed management and habitat benefits.

America significantly under-utilizes biomass and biogas for electricity production. Sweden already gets one-third of its electricity from biomass. Biomass can do everything that coal does, and do it without adding greenhouse gases to the atmosphere, as long as the biomass is harvested sustainably. Biomass is carbon that was just taken out of the atmosphere. Coal is carbon that was taken out of the atmosphere hundreds of millions of years ago. We need to stop burning coal and use biomass instead.

In addition to woody biomass, we can harvest annual energy crops or the sustainable portion of crop residue from farm fields for electrical production. Burning energy crops or crop residues for electricity does not add carbon dioxide to the atmosphere. The carbon in the energy crops was just taken out of the atmosphere when the crops were growing and would be released back to the atmosphere when the plants decompose. We must also capture methane from landfills to slow down the buildup of that greenhouse gas and to use it, instead, to generate heat and electricity.

Renewable electricity is even better when it is combined with industrial co-generation, where industries that produce and use heat or steam also generate electricity. Industrial co-generation can be done with biomass or biogas. If there are places where the use of biomass or biogas is not practical, industries could co-generate burning natural gas, at least in the short run, because natural gas is cleaner than coal and co-generation is so highly energy-efficient it would still reduce the carbon footprint of the plant. Soon, however, we need to leave all of the natural gas in the ground, too.

The primary purpose of implementing 100% renewable electricity is to meet our obligations for reducing greenhouse gases. Of course, it will also create jobs. Dirty fossil fuel projects can also create some jobs, at least in the short run, but renewable electricity creates more jobs. Job creation is a significant benefit from a 100% homegrown renewable electricity strategy.

A growing number of homeowners and businesses are already installing renewable electrical generation. I support that, but the most important action you can take is to advocate for state and national policies that move us to 100% renewable electricity by 2030. We need policies to:

- Make the production tax credit for renewable electricity permanent.
- Require utilities to connect renewable generators to the grid.
- Guarantee minimum payments to renewable electricity producers.
- Increase minimum renewable energy requirements for utilities.
- Make new infrastructure investments for transmission of renewable electricity.

Production tax credits which reward actual production of renewable energy should be made permanent, not because the industry "needs subsidies," but because the public should provide ongoing incentives to reflect the climate, health, environmental, and national security benefits of clean, homegrown renewable electricity. Thanks to the incentive of the production tax credit, wind power is now able to generate more electricity at lower wind speeds. Making the production tax credit permanent would encourage more job growth in the renewable electricity industry and spur even more technological innovation.

Requiring utilities to connect renewable generators to the grid and guaranteeing minimum payments (sometimes called "feed-in tariffs") would unleash the market to provide a rapid expansion of renewable electricity. Germany (with much less sunshine than America) is using feed-in tariffs to expand its solar industry. It is on course to meet one-third of its electrical demand with solar.

Increasing our renewable electricity standards would ensure that we make progress toward 100% renewable electricity. New investments in transmission infrastructure would create jobs and bring large-scale renewable electricity to market.

Again, we need comprehensive national climate policy to put an increasing price on carbon pollution so that all Americans have an incentive for renewable electricity. With your support we can adopt policies to achieve 100% renewable electricity by 2030.

Transportation Solutions

Fossil fuel use and greenhouse gas emissions in transportation can be reduced in a number of ways. In addition to driving and flying less and getting better gas mileage, we need to rebuild our communities for the new energy and climate reality. We need walkable, bike-able, and transit-friendly communities.

If you are thinking about building or buying into a new development on the outskirts of an urban area, think about how people are going to get to work and school when gas is $5 a gallon or more. Given the new energy and climate reality, the better course is to re-develop our main streets, revitalize our downtown neighborhoods, and make sure all new development encourages walking, biking, and public transportation.

We need plug-in hybrids to take us to the next level of fuel efficiency and fuel savings. Owners of the Chevy Volt tell me they are getting more than 80 miles per gallon, even with long-distance travel between cities. We need to support the move toward electric vehicles with new charging stations and other electric vehicle infrastructure. As we move toward 100% renewable electricity by 2030, we can charge electric vehicles basically for free when the wind is blowing and the sun is shining. Even without 100% renewable electricity, electric vehicles are so efficient that they reduce greenhouse gas emissions compared to gasoline-powered cars.

We need to restore rail lines across the country for not only passenger rail, but also freight rail. According to the Association of American Railroads, rail reduces greenhouse gas emissions in shipping by two-thirds or more compared to truck transportation. As air travel and heavy trucking decline because of rising oil prices and the need to reduce greenhouse gases, we need a vibrant rail network to help businesses and individuals maintain mobility.

The next generation of biofuels (ethanol and biodiesel) that are made from plant materials other than corn and soybeans can also help reduce greenhouse gases. I have supported the creation of bio-refineries in Iowa that will literally make fuel, animal feed, plastic substitutes, and other advanced industrial materials out of crop residues. However, we cannot biofuel our way out of the global warming problem. Biofuels are at best a part of a comprehensive strategy for transportation solutions in the climate century.

These transportation solutions do not mean our economy will suffer. To the contrary, they have the potential to create millions of jobs, save billions of dollars in energy costs, and make our families and communities more prosperous. We can slash our current energy bills and keep dollars here in America by reducing gasoline consumption and building walkable, bike-able, and transit-friendly communities. We can avoid shipping costs and greenhouse gas emissions by shopping locally. We can take staycations at or near home, rather than flying to remote destinations and taking our dollars with us. At work, we can cut costs and save time by using teleconferencing instead of air travel.

> Transportation solutions have the potential to create millions of jobs, save billions of dollars in energy costs, and make us more prosperous.

Public policy will play an enormous role in promoting transportation solutions. Local government needs to play a major role in land use decisions that promote sustainability and greenhouse gas reductions. Government at the federal and state level needs to restore rail lines across the country. Government at all levels needs to control spending on new highways in favor of re-investment in main streets, downtown revitalization, and transit solutions.

Government policy needs to encourage electric vehicles, charging stations, and the grid improvements that will make electric vehicles even more attractive than they already are. Comprehensive climate policy that puts an increasing price on carbon pollution would encourage all of these transportation solutions compared to our current fossil fuel-intensive transportation system.

Because public policy is so important for transportation solutions in the climate century, so is your work as a citizen to educate the public and advocate with elected officials for climate action.

Local and Healthy Foods

Another solution in the climate century is producing and buying local and healthy foods. Consumers can reduce the energy use and greenhouse gas emissions embedded in their food by eating local to reduce food transportation, by eating at home to reduce the energy used in the food service industry, and by eating lower on the food chain. Such actions will also help local agricultural producers and help build stronger and more vibrant communities.

We need to support better agricultural policies and practices. We need to reduce nitrogen fertilizer use to cut nitrous oxide emissions, clean up our water, and reduce hypoxia in the Gulf of Mexico. We need better manure management to reduce methane emissions and capture methane for electricity. We need tillage practices and land management to control soil erosion, improve water quality, and sequester carbon.

Another reason we need to eat and live healthier is so that we can free up resources to be used for fighting global warming. As we get healthier, we will spend less on health care and have more money to invest in reducing greenhouse gas emissions and mitigating future climate disasters.

Research, Development, and Deployment

All of the climate actions I have discussed so far to reduce greenhouse gas emissions are based on existing technology. We do not need to wait for "nuclear fusion" or some other exotic "technological fix" to save us. In fact, any money we spend on so-called "solutions" like that are a waste of money we should be investing in today's technologies to create jobs and move us beyond fossil fuels. We can slash our greenhouse gas emissions sufficiently today – through existing public policy options, proven technologies, and positive voluntary lifestyle changes – to make the climate safe for future generations.

Yet, we should also invest significantly in the research, development, and deployment of new technologies that are realistic and targeted toward reducing greenhouse gas emissions. Technological innovation holds the promise of not only making it easier for Americans to slash our greenhouse gas emissions, but we can also use that technology to help other countries slash their emissions, too. Like President Reagan proposed sharing the Strategic Defense Initiative with the Soviet Union, we should share our technological research for greenhouse gas reductions with other countries out of our own national self-interests.

Some of the promising areas of research include better vehicle fuel efficiency, better building energy efficiency, renewable electricity, electrical storage, transmission improvements, transportation solutions like high-speed rail and the next generation of biofuels, and sustainable industrial practices. These areas of research and development all hold the promise of more rapid greenhouse gas reductions and more prosperity in the future.

Climate Preparedness

In the climate century, even as we slash our greenhouse gas emissions, we need to get ready for more climate disasters. It starts with ecosystem monitoring so that we can identify and anticipate changes that are underway. We should support the people whose jobs are to monitor our environment and inform the public about climate change. However, monitoring alone is far from enough.

We also need to restore our prairies and our forests with native species that are likely to survive the coming climatic changes. Prairies and forests not only provide ecosystem services like clean water and clean air, they also sequester carbon dioxide and provide biomass and biogas fuel as an alternative to coal.

Investments in natural resources also provide habitat for game species and other recreational opportunities and will help preserve biodiversity for future generations. We need natural corridors so that native plants and wildlife will be able to survive the additional warming and climatic change in the coming decades. We need to find ways to connect the parks and preserves we have scattered across the landscape so that as climate changes, native plants and wildlife will have a chance to move with those changes.

We need better water and watershed management, both to reduce future flood damage and to ameliorate drought conditions. Wetlands, buffer strips, detention basins, rain gardens, and rain water harvesting will allow regions to manage water better.

We should ask citizens to play a positive role in combating droughts and floods. During the floods in Iowa in 2008, volunteers turned out by the thousands to help sandbag buildings to protect them from flood damage. We need that same sense of teamwork and enthusiasm for the good of our community before the next disaster hits. I call it the "spirit of the sandbag." Citizens can use rain barrels, rain gardens, vegetated buffer strips, and wetlands to manage extreme precipitation and flooding. Citizens can insist that floodplains are set aside to accommodate floodwaters, and that any development near creeks and rivers be flood-proof, so we can reduce future flood damage.

We also need to provide citizens with a clear message about what can be done to help ameliorate the devastation from drought. Many of the solutions to prevent future flooding will also help ameliorate drought. We can conserve water and harvest more of the rain that falls. We need to fix leaks and adopt low-flow technologies. We can save our greywater to help water young trees and gardens.

We also need tornado and hurricane safe buildings including safe rooms in every building and every mobile home park. Regardless of whether climate change is the cause of more intense tornadoes and hurricanes, we need to stop the carnage that occurs when tornadoes and hurricanes hit.

Public policy has done woefully little to support pre-disaster hazard mitigation. In the climate century, hazard mitigation should move from being a minor part of local, state, and federal government to being a core function. According to Iowa's Homeland Security and Emergency Management Agency, the limited hazard mitigation investments that have been made in our state have already avoided more than $2 in damage for every dollar spent, and those mitigation investments remain in place to guard against future disasters.

Just like government provides police protection and fire departments, government should provide hazard mitigation. I support police and firefighters in their jobs because I believe that public safety is government's first responsibility. I am personally willing to pay higher taxes to support police and fire protection. We need citizens to add hazard mitigation to the core public safety functions of government.

Finally, we need to support disaster relief organizations like the United Way, the American Red Cross, and faith-based relief organizations. Those groups did an incredible job when Cedar Rapids flooded, both with emergency relief and long-term recovery. As the number of disasters increases, Americans run the risk of suffering from disaster fatigue. Instead of disaster fatigue, we need disaster endurance. In the climate century, it is our job to help prevent disasters and to help the victims of those disasters that cannot be avoided.

Chapter Seven
Politics and Climate

In the climate century, the fight against climate change needs to take its place as our new national purpose, just like winning World War II and the Cold War were America's national purpose during my parents' generation.

Americans are ready to do just that. America's scientific leaders have repeatedly called for climate action. Business leaders support climate action. Faith leaders support climate action. In our military, there are increasing numbers of "climate patriots" who know we need to fight climate change to safeguard our country's national self-interests. Grassroots support for climate action is rapidly increasing. In every family, more people see themselves as "climate parents" or "grannies for a livable future." After the heat and drought of 2012, after Hurricane Sandy, after so many recent climate disasters, Americans are ready for national climate action.

What we have been missing – and what we now urgently need – are strong national leaders who can pull the country together to slash greenhouse gas emissions, safeguard our people and our property in the face of growing climate disasters, and lead the world into a new global alliance for sustainability.

Economics and Climate

The central issue in today's politics in the United States has been the economy, or, as elected officials like to say, "jobs, jobs, jobs." Many political leaders currently believe that even if climate is a problem, it has to remain secondary to what they perceive as a higher priority, job creation. This focus on short-term job creation without regard to its climate impact is badly flawed.

The source of our current economic problems is largely the cost of imported foreign oil, well over $200 billion drained every year since 2006 from our economy for the same amount of oil we imported in the 1990s at a cost of less than $60 billion a year. High fossil fuel energy costs are a brake on our economy and are preventing a more robust recovery.

In Iowa, our total energy expenditures have grown from $5.5 billion in 1998 to $13.8 billion in 2011 – a growth rate of 7.5% per year over 13 years or from less than $2,000 per Iowan in 1998 to more than $4,500 per Iowan in 2011. The biggest cause of that increase has been motor fuels, which have grown from $2.2 billion in 1998 to $8.3 billion in 2011 – a growth rate of nearly 11% per year.

Our economy is also sluggish because of high health costs caused by coal and other fossil fuels, and because of climate-related disasters. Another example from Iowa: The floods that resulted in 15 presidential disaster declarations in Iowa since 1990 have cost Iowans more than $20 billion, or more than $6,000 per Iowan.

The Drought of 2012 was another billion-dollar disaster for Iowa. Nationally, disaster costs were $52 billion in 2011, and Hurricane Sandy alone cost more than $70 billion. Failing to address climate change will commit us irreversibly to higher levels of disaster damage and health costs in the future.

Proposals like the Keystone "Export" pipeline may create a few temporary jobs, but they would also continue global dependence on expensive foreign oil and commit the earth to even higher levels of warming and more climate disasters in the future. Trying to create jobs through investments in dirty energy will only exacerbate the costs of imported oil, health costs, and climate disasters, ruining our economy in the process. We can create more jobs in the short run with investments in energy efficiency and renewable energy than we can through investments in dirty energy, and our clean energy investments will save us money in the long run.

We can create jobs through fuel-efficient vehicles, electric vehicles, and better electric vehicle infrastructure that will save consumers billions in energy costs by using those vehicles.

We can create jobs by building or rebuilding rail lines and modern new rail cars. In the future, these rail systems will provide affordable transportation regardless of future oil increases.

We can create jobs by retrofitting buildings for green practices, building new green buildings, and revitalizing downtowns and main streets across the country. Once completed, those projects will continue to save consumers billions in energy costs by lowering energy use and reducing the need for transportation.

We can create jobs by promoting renewable energy. Once built, wind and solar have no ongoing fuel costs, but require workers to maintain the equipment. Wind and solar mean lower fuel costs, more job creation.

We can create jobs by building infrastructure to withstand extreme weather and by investing in natural resources and watershed management. Once built, these projects and practices will provide confidence for investors and save taxpayers billions when future disasters hit.

The only way to fix the economy in the short-run, and

lay the foundation for long-term economic prosperity, is to invest in sustainable technologies that create jobs, save consumers money, and minimize long-term disaster damage.

Business and Climate

Some people think that climate action will be bad for business. In fact, many business leaders support climate action. Groups like the U.S. Climate Action Partnership and the Business Environmental Leadership Council have expressed strong support for national climate action. Numerous entrepreneurs in clean energy businesses, involved in renewable energy trade associations and advocacy groups like the Small Business Majority, also understand that climate action is good for business. The sooner our country starts taking climate action, the better it will be for American business.

In 2007, I was the chair of a legislative committee on energy efficiency aimed at developing new policies to promote energy efficiency in Iowa. Iowa has had a good history of energy efficiency, leading the nation in utility energy efficiency program spending per capita, but that is not good enough for the climate century. During those meetings, one Iowa employer, Whirlpool, told my committee that energy efficiency is the "quickest, cheapest, cleanest, and most secure" way to meet energy demand. Whirlpool can create jobs and build wealth by selling energy-efficient Energy Star appliances. Taking climate action to improve energy efficiency helps Whirlpool's business.

Not all business leaders embraced energy efficiency at our meetings. An executive from the Alcoa plant in Iowa spoke against making large industries pay for utility energy efficiency programs based on his claim that large industries had already done everything possible to optimize energy efficiency. This executive argued that energy efficiency programs are basically a tax on large industries to make them pay for energy efficiency programs to help other customers.

I was disappointed with his presentation. We know industries can do more to save energy. We also know that energy efficiency programs avoid the costs of new power plants to help keep rates low for all customers, including large industries. In Iowa, it is estimated that our energy efficiency programs over 20 years have allowed Iowa utilities to avoid the construction of at least two large base-load power plants, helping keep our electrical rates lower than the national average and saving consumers billions.

After the meeting, however, I was shocked to discover that Alcoa was one of the companies in the U.S. Climate Action Partnership. In other words, what Alcoa's representative in Iowa told us did not match its national position. It turned out he did not know about it.

As part of the Climate Action Partnership, Alcoa had called for stronger energy efficiency policies and comprehensive climate legislation designed to establish a "mandatory emission reduction pathway" to reduce greenhouse gas emissions 60-80% below current levels by 2050. In addition to Alcoa, some of the other businesses in the Climate Action Partnership include Caterpillar, Chrysler Jeep Dodge, Dow Chemical, DuPont, Ford, General Electric, General Motors, Honeywell, Johnson & Johnson, PepsiCo, Siemens, and Xerox.

I wish the Alcoa representative had been able to tell us about the Climate Action Partnership at our committee hearing. It would have helped educate Iowans that businesses do support climate action to reduce greenhouse gas emissions. It would have helped us pass stronger energy efficiency legislation. Instead, we ended up passing legislation that asked our utilities to study the potential for further voluntary energy savings. I was pleased to floor manage that bill, and to make some progress, but we could have done more. In the climate century, we need to do more.

Like the Climate Action Partnership, the Business

Environmental Leadership Council also recommends "economy-wide, mandatory approaches" for reducing greenhouse gas emissions. The Council's members include Bank of America, Bayer, HP, IBM, Intel, Johnson Controls, and Weyerhaeuser.

Unfortunately, I do not think Americans know there is such strong business support for climate action. I wish these businesses would do more to educate Americans about their support for climate action. We need more business leaders who will not only sign up for climate action, but also will speak up and actually lobby our Congressional representatives and Senators for climate action.

However, the list of businesses that have signed up does show that climate action is not inherently "bad for business." If we unite in favor of climate action, we can actually create jobs, help businesses expand, and increase future prosperity.

We do need to be careful not to reduce greenhouse gases in the United States by simply driving large industrial energy consumers to other countries. That is one of the reasons why we need a strong climate-centered foreign policy. It is also why consumers need to support greenhouse gas reducing products and technologies, so businesses can succeed as they move away from fossil fuels.

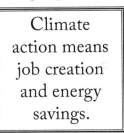

Climate action means job creation and energy savings.

Beyond these efforts, we need to assist workers and industries that would be harmed by climate action. Climate action will necessarily reduce coal mining and drilling for gas and oil and require other changes in our economy. The sooner we get started, and the more certain our policies are for reducing greenhouse gas emissions, the quicker businesses and workers can adjust.

Personally, I would be willing to re-prioritize the budget to make sure that dislocated workers get the training and assistance they need to make the transition. After all, climate change is not their fault – their purpose in mining coal and drilling for oil and gas was not to change the climate – and we are all in this fight together. It is time for Americans to unite behind climate action.

Freedom and Climate

Like those who are concerned about the effect of climate action on the economy, there are those who are concerned that climate action will interfere with our freedom. We Americans rightly treasure our freedom. The biggest threat to that freedom is not climate action, but rather the chaos that occurs after climate disasters. When our government takes action to fight climate change, it promotes freedom.

For a few days after the Flood of 2008 in Cedar Rapids, I lived for what I hope will be the only time in my life behind a National Guard checkpoint. Floodwaters inundated much of the neighborhood where I live. To protect flooded properties while residents were under a mandatory evacuation order, the Iowa National Guard was mobilized and checkpoints were established to guard the entrances to flooded neighborhoods. When I left my home the first morning after the checkpoint was established, I made sure I had photo identification and an overnight bag.

I was grateful for the presence of the men and women who serve in the Iowa National Guard. They helped prevent any loss of life or theft during the flood. At the same time, I had an uneasy feeling about what it meant for the future. During disasters, people are often willing to give up some of their freedom in exchange for security. In the coming decades, as people experience more frequent

> Strong climate action is necessary to ensure freedom in the climate century.

and severe climate disasters, will we be willing to give up more and more of our freedom in exchange for security?

Two of the leading deniers of climate science, Fred Singer and Dennis Avery, wrote in their book, *Unstoppable Global Warming* (2007), that if we become convinced that the earth is warming to "dangerous levels due to human-emitted greenhouse gases, public policy will then have to evaluate such potential remedies as banning autos and air conditioners." This was a scare tactic on their part to try to discourage climate action.

Nowhere in this book have I proposed banning automobiles or air conditioners. Those are not the only options, nor are they good options. In fact, they are terrible options. However, if we wait too long, and we are in a climate emergency, then those types of options might become necessary.

In the past, our country has adopted draconian policies like the suspension of habeas corpus (Civil War), restrictions on free speech (World War I), and forced internment of citizens of Japanese origin (World War II). Even our court system, the guardian of our liberty, has upheld those deprivations of freedom because of emergency situations. If we face increasingly rapid warming and widespread devastation from climate disasters in the decades ahead, would Americans consider restrictions on population growth or human mobility?

To protect and promote human freedom in the climate century, we need to take strong climate action now to limit global warming and mitigate future climate disasters.

Faith and Climate

Some people disregard the science of climate change because they believe God will not allow the earth to be ruined. That type of "blind faith" is misplaced and ignores terrible things that have happened in human history. It is really an excuse to avoid personal responsibility. Other people disregard the science of climate change because they believe God is punishing people on earth. That type of "fatalism" also ignores personal responsibility.

My faith tells me something very different about global warming and climate change. It tells me that God loves us, but that human selfishness and greed can do much harm. It tells me we should be stewards of God's creation. It tells me we have a responsibility to our neighbors across the street and around the world. It tells me we have a responsibility for future generations, too.

I had the opportunity to coordinate a global warming project for Ecumenical Ministries of Iowa for six months before the presidential precinct caucuses in Iowa in 2000. In connection with this job, I had to articulate why people of faith should be involved on this issue. One answer was simple: People of faith are called to use our knowledge and intelligence to protect God's creation and to protect God's children from the adverse effects of climate change. God has given us dominion over the earth, a word meaning stewardship, not exploitation; preservation, not destruction.

It also occurred to me that in our common faith tradition, we have already heard the story of climate change in the story of Joseph in Egypt from the Book of Genesis.

Joseph, a Hebrew slave in prison, was asked to read Pharaoh's dreams. Based on those dreams, Joseph determined that there would be seven years of plenty followed by seven years of drought. The Pharaoh put Joseph in charge of the country and quickly Joseph took action. He imposed a twenty percent tax on all agricultural production during the years of plenty to build up enormous reserves of grain.

There must have been Egyptians who were skeptical of a Hebrew inmate taxing their grain production when times were so good. Nevertheless, Joseph knew that it would be too late if they waited for the drought to happen. With God's help, he was able to take action. Because of his actions, when the drought hit, Egypt survived, along with Joseph's family, who fled to Egypt as environmental refugees.

In November 1999, twenty religious leaders in Iowa issued a joint statement on global warming that I helped draft. Here is what they said:

> As we face the challenge of global warming, we are called once again to re-affirm our commitment to be responsible stewards of God's creation, to act in love toward our neighbors around the world, and to deepen our relationship with God our Creator.
>
> Leading scientists have warned us that, sooner or later, our continued use of fossil fuels and continued deforestation will disrupt the relatively stable climate with which we have been blessed. The resulting changes in weather would threaten our environment, our health and safety, our economy, our agriculture, and our security. As Iowans, we especially understand the blessings of good land and the relatively predictable climate that God has bestowed upon us, and our responsibility to be stewards of God's creation.
>
> Like Joseph in Egypt, who read Pharaoh's dreams to use seven good years of plenty to prepare Egypt for seven years of drought, we are now called to take responsible precautionary action to limit global warming to the extent possible and to prepare for the climatic changes that cannot be avoided.

Iowa's religious leaders called on people of faith to provide leadership on the climate issue. As they explained, "Because of our relationship with God, we have the freedom, the strength, and the hope to change lifestyles and policies that endanger our future and future generations."

Iowa's religious leaders have continued to express their support for climate action, by starting Iowa Interfaith Power & Light in 2005, by running a Cool Congregations program to help congregations reduce their energy use, and by issuing yet another call for climate action in April 2012.

It is not just religious leaders in Iowa who support climate action. Groups like the National Religious Partnership for the Environment, the national Interfaith Power & Light, the Evangelical Environmental Network, Young Evangelicals for Climate Action, and the Evangelical Climate Initiative are all providing leadership to support national climate action.

In this era of interest group politics, political action committees, and Super PACs, people of faith may have a unique ability to think and act globally and inter-generationally. As Pope Benedict XVI said about climate, we owe "solidarity" to "those living in the poorer areas of the world and to future generations." In February 2011, the United States Catholic Conference Department of Justice, Peace and Human Development said:

> The impacts of climate change – including increased temperatures, rising sea levels, and changes in rainfall that contribute to more frequent and severe droughts – are making the lives of the world's poorest even more precarious. Urgent action that both addresses the growing impact of climate change and acts to protect the poor and vulnerable is needed.

There is very little that is more important for people of faith than to get involved in education and advocacy for climate action. Climate change is a reality. It is already hurting millions of people in the United States and around the world. We have a moral duty to help those affected by climate disasters.

The number of people hurt by climate disasters will grow significantly unless we change public policy, slash greenhouse gas emissions, and prepare for future extreme weather. Like Joseph, we cannot be afraid to use the power of government to safeguard people and property from future climate disasters. Like Joseph, we cannot wait for the disaster before we take action.

America's Natural Heritage

As Americans unite behind climate action as our new national purpose, we can also draw upon our national heritage to support our efforts. From the times of the frontier to current times, we have always understood that our purpose is to provide a better future for the next generation. Mistakes have been made along the way, but ultimately Americans have done what is right on the great moral challenges of our times – the abolishment of slavery, the establishment of civil rights, and the victories in World War II and the Cold War.

The great moral challenge today is to find a way for seven or more billion people to live on the earth sustainably in the climate century and beyond. As the world's leading country, the United States has a special role to play in this effort. Fortunately, our history shows us that Americans can take the action we need to preserve and protect our natural heritage for future generations.

Over the centuries, Americans have loved and revered nature. Daniel Boone knew that nature was a "series of wonders." Lewis, Clark, and Sacagawea undertook the common enterprise known as the Corps of Discovery. Thoreau "went to the woods" to make sure he really lived. Chief Seattle recognized we were just a single thread in the "web of life." Like the Iroquois people, "we must consider the impact of our decisions on the next seven generations."

In the late 19th Century, Americans began to recognize the need to preserve our natural treasures for future generations. We took action and set aside national parks like Yellowstone for permanent protection.

At the start of the 20th Century, Republican President Teddy Roosevelt, a great outdoorsman and conservationist, loved and revered nature. Once, as President, he camped out for three nights under the open skies in Yosemite Park with the founder of the Sierra Club, John Muir, waking up one morning covered by several inches of snow. Roosevelt helped expand America's national parks, leading to the establishment of the National Park Service in 1916.

During the Dust Bowl and Great Depression, leaders like Hugh Bennett and Ding Darling, the editorial cartoonist for the *Des Moines Register*, helped usher in a new era of public assistance for private land conservation. Their accomplishments included the creation of the Soil Conservation Service and the Fish and Wildlife Service. In that same era, Iowa native Aldo Leopold wrote *The Sand County Almanac* and brought "the land ethic" to America.

In the generation after World War II, leaders like Rachel Carson pointed out the growing threats to the natural world from pollution. The first Earth Day in 1970 both reflected growing environmental awareness and contributed to the growth of the environmental movement. Congress continued to protect our natural heritage through laws like the Wilderness Act of 1964, the Wild and Scenic Rivers Act of 1968, the National Environmental Policy Act of 1969, the Clean Air Act of 1970, the Clean Water Act of 1972, and the Endangered Species Act of 1973.

In the 1980s, President Reagan signed the Montreal Protocol to protect the earth's ozone layer from ozone-depleting gases. The first President Bush strengthened the Montreal Protocol, and signed the Clean Air Act Amendments of 1990 to combat acid rain. He also signed the United Nations Framework Convention on Climate Change in 1992 that promised to avoid "dangerous anthropogenic interference" with the earth's climate system.

Since the first Earth Day, a growing number of Americans have been engaged in significant voluntary efforts to reduce consumption, reduce waste, and preserve and protect important natural areas in our communities.

Now it is time for all of us to draw upon this heritage and take up the fight against climate change. It is no longer enough to "think globally and act locally." In the climate century, we Americans have the responsibility and opportunity to take the climate action we need – locally, nationally, and internationally – to protect our natural heritage from the dangers of climate change. Like the Americans who have acted before us, I am confident we will do the job.

Climate Parents and Climate Patriots

There is growing recognition that Americans owe it to the next generation to win the fight against climate change. As parents and grandparents, we care about our children, and so we need to care about climate change. In the same way that we invest our time and treasure in their education, health, and well being, we need to invest in a clean energy future and infrastructure that safeguards against future climate disasters.

One group that is promoting this message is "Climate Parents," formed by Lisa Hoyos and Mark Hertsgaard, the author of *Hot: Living Through the Next Fifty Years on Earth* (2011). Another group is "100 Grannies for a Livable Future," formed by the Rev. Barbara Schlachter and other grandmothers in Iowa. These groups reflect the growing commitment by parents and grandparents to fight climate change for today's children and future generations.

These groups are just two of the literally hundreds if not thousands of grassroots organizations in cities and regions across the country trying to rally support for climate action. In Iowa, community groups like Green Dubuque, Sustainable Independence, Iowa City Climate Advocates,

Transition Des Moines, and the Indianola Green Team are promoting climate action.

National efforts like Citizens Climate Lobby and 350.org are relatively new to the cause, while established environmental groups like the Sierra Club, the National Wildlife Federation, the Natural Resources Defense Council, the Union of Concerned Scientists, and the Environmental Defense Fund continue to push for climate action. The momentum for climate action is growing.

Even our retired military leaders are getting involved. Dennis McGinn, a retired vice admiral in the United States Navy, now serves as president and chief executive officer of the American Council on Renewable Energy. He spoke in Iowa in October 2011 about the recognition by military leaders of the urgent need to combat climate change for national security reasons. In 2010, he prepared a video with former Secretary of the Navy and former Republican Senator John Warner of Virginia, and other retired military officials, entitled "Climate Patriots." In the video, McGinn states it is patriotic to conserve energy and use renewable energy resources to reduce the threat of disasters and political instability associated with climate change.

Military leaders know climate action will improve our security.

"Climate Parents," "Climate Patriots," and all of these groups are signs of growing support for climate action.

Strong Political Leaders for Climate Action

What we need now are strong national political leaders who can pull the country together behind the climate action that is so urgently needed. We could debate why America's political leaders have so far failed to provide the needed action, but after the heat and drought of 2012, after

Hurricane Sandy, and after all of the other recent climate disasters, let's just leave that for future historians. For now, we need climate action.

Here is what strong national political leaders should do: Tell the American people the truth about climate change. Stand up to the interest groups that seek to extract short-term profits at the long-term cost of more climate disasters. Hold accountable those elected officials who continue to deny climate change.

We need leaders who can inspire Americans to participate in a national effort to fight climate change. We need leaders who will use government as a tool to take the necessary action to safeguard people and property from future climate disasters. We need leaders who will unleash the power of market forces behind clean, homegrown renewable energy. We need leaders who will stand up to China, Russia, India, and the other major carbon polluters, demand mutually verified reductions in greenhouse gas emissions, and create a new global alliance for sustainability.

Global warming is a problem. Let's get going. Let's innovate. Let's fight for the next generation. Let's support those political leaders who vote for climate action. Let's take climate action.

Some people say America cannot do it anymore. Don't believe that for a second. America has always been able to shake off its self-doubt to lead the world to do great things. In his book, *Freedom From Fear*, historian David Kennedy tells the story that before the United States entered World War II, President Roosevelt wanted to order 15,000 aircraft, but the Army Air Force chief of staff asked, "What are we going to do with fifteen thousand planes?" Five years later, the United States had built over 300,000 aircraft, won the war, and preserved freedom for the world.

We can still take the bold action we need to fight climate change if we are determined, compassionate, innovative, and inspired:

- Let's slash our energy use through energy efficiency and energy conservation.
- Let's produce 100% renewable electricity by 2030.
- Let's make every new and renovated building a green building.
- Let's build electric vehicles and an electric vehicle infrastructure.
- Let's rebuild rail.
- Let's revitalize our downtowns and main streets.
- Let's grow local, healthy foods.
- Let's prepare our cities, our watersheds, and our states so we can survive the climate disasters of the future.
- Let's lead the world to slash greenhouse gas emissions and keep our climate safe for future generations.

In the climate century, this is our national purpose.

National Climate Policy

In the climate century, every elected official at every level of government – city, county, state, and federal – has a role to play in the fight against global warming and the climate changes that can no longer be avoided.

Cities, counties, and states have a job to do mitigating future climate disasters, reducing energy use, and promoting renewable energy. For example, in Iowa, I have proposed a ten-year, $600 million state investment in hazard mitigation and watershed management to help my state ameliorate future droughts and say "never again" to the level of flood damage we suffered in 2008.

I also support an initiative called Iowa Renewable Energy Jobs 2020 that would increase the amount of electricity we produce from renewable energy from 20% today to at least 40% by 2020, create an additional 20,000 clean energy jobs, and save consumers at least $1 billion a year in energy costs through energy efficiency and fuel efficiency. By adopting this initiative, Iowa could demonstrate to the world that a modern economy can be even more prosperous using fewer fossil fuels.

To deal with a global issue like climate change, however, we must have strong national policy and American leadership on a global basis. There is no greater hope for the future than the United States of America.

After the heat and drought of 2012, after Hurricane Sandy, after all of the other recent climate disasters, there must be something that Congress could do to address climate change. A do-something Congress would do something on climate change. Here are eight actions Congress could take to help fight climate change now:

1. **Make the renewable energy production tax credit permanent** – The federal production tax credit was extended for one year in the fiscal cliff compromise. Congress should make it permanent to reflect the climate, health, and security benefits of homegrown renewable energy. This would preserve and create tens of thousands of jobs and foster innovation and long-term success for our renewable energy industries.

2. **End billions of dollars in fossil fuel subsidies** – These subsidies are not only encouraging more greenhouse gas emissions, they are increasing our deficit and depriving us of the resources we need now, and will need in the future, to fight climate change.

3. **Stop the Keystone "Export" pipeline** – This pipeline would increase global dependence on the dirty tar sands of Canada, and would also endanger America's water, wildlife, and values, by condemning American farms and ranches for a pipeline to take foreign oil across America to Port Arthur, Texas, for sale on the global market.

4. **Stop oil drilling in the Arctic Ocean** – This oil should be left permanently in the ground for climate reasons, and the Arctic should be permanently protected from the dangers of oil spills.

5. **Apply greenhouse gas standards to existing coal plants** – Existing coal plants should not be exempt from greenhouse gas regulations under the Clean Air Act. Making existing coal plants comply would reduce greenhouse gas pollution and prevent outdated coal plants from blocking the development of homegrown renewable electricity.

6. **End clean water and clear air exemptions for fracking** – Hydraulic fracturing, or fracking, should not be exempt from clean water and clean air regulations. It is endangering water supplies and is increasing our dependence on fossil fuels.

7. **Adopt a carbon tax or revenue-neutral carbon fee and dividend** – These proposals would put a price on carbon, which is needed to signal businesses and consumers to move away from fossil fuels toward clean energy solutions. Whether Congress wants to use the revenue to reduce the deficit or reward people who reduce their carbon emissions through a per citizen dividend, we need a price on carbon.

8. **Help states and localities prepare for future climate disasters** – Our country can provide help to states, cities, and counties through federal infrastructure and pre-disaster hazard mitigation programs, and by investing in our natural resources to give native wildlife and plants a chance to survive the changing climate.

Many groups have worked on a number of versions of comprehensive climate legislation. In 2003, there was the McCain-Lieberman Climate Stewardship Act. In 2009, there was Waxman-Markey or the American Climate Energy Security Act. There are general concepts like cap-and-trade, carbon tax, cap-tax-and-trade, or car-bon-fee-and-dividend. It is less important which version Congress passes, than it is to pass one. The growing dangers of climate change require that Congress act and pass comprehensive climate legislation as soon as possible.

Citizens need to lead the way by advocating with our Congressional representatives and Senators to support climate action. Even if a Congressional representative or Senator has not supported climate action in the past, citizens should still advocate for climate action. After the heat and drought of 2012, after Hurricane Sandy, and after all of the other recent climate disasters, some elected officials will change their minds. A "Doubting Thomas" today can be a leader for climate action tomorrow. However, if they still do not support climate action, then we need to find candidates to replace them.

Climate Foreign Policy

As the fight against climate change becomes our new national purpose, it will also take its place at the center of American foreign policy. Climate change is a global threat, and addressing it will require American leadership on a global basis. To deal effectively with climate change, America needs to lead the world in a new global alliance for sustainability. Our climate foreign policy must address the need to reduce emissions globally and the economic, humanitarian, and security risks associated with future climate disasters around the world.

Unfortunately, our climate foreign policy has so far been a failure. In the 1990s, the U.S. Senate voted unanimously to oppose any international climate treaty that did not include developing countries, especially China and India. The Senate ignored the fact that America was – and continues to be – the largest producer of greenhouse gases on a per capita basis. Moreover, the fact that China and India have wanted to grow their economies using fossil fuels makes the fight against climate change more urgent, not less urgent. We need America to lead the world to combat climate change. But rather than getting China and India more involved in the international fight against climate change, American foreign policy has used China and India as an excuse for inaction.

By our inaction, we are now rapidly approaching the brink of climate disaster. Globally, we are burning more coal, more oil, and more natural gas than ever before. A headline from the Associated Press on November 4, 2011, summed it up: "Biggest jump ever seen in global warming gases."

Our lack of leadership is also putting America in danger of losing the clean energy technologies that could solve the problem in the future. According to the Worldwatch Institute, China now leads the world in global investment in renewable energy – more than $52 billion in 2011. India now leads the world in terms of growth in renewable energy investment – a 62% growth rate in 2011. Although America was still second in overall renewable energy investment, our relative position continues to slide compared to other countries.

Rather than waiting for China and India to lead the world, America should lead the world into a new global alliance for sustainability. America should pull the world's largest emitters of greenhouse gases together to form a new global alliance. Along with the United States, China, Europe, India, Russia, and Japan account for approximately 70% of the world's greenhouse gas emissions. Here is what the new global alliance would strive to do:

1. **Mutual Emission Reductions** – Each country would commit to different but declining limits on greenhouse gas emissions, with incentives for every country to reduce their emissions even more.

2. **Technology Development** – Each country would commit to increasing its investment in research, development, and deployment of renewable energy and other sustainable technologies, and sharing its technology with others in the alliance. America should lead the world in the research, development, and deployment of the technologies that can slash greenhouse gas emissions. Like President Reagan proposed sharing the Strategic Defense Initiative with the Soviet Union, we should share technology based on our own national self-interests.

3. **Geoengineering** – Geoengineering is the concept that humans may someday try to manage directly the earth's climate to mitigate the effects of climate change. It is unproven and highly dangerous, and is presently unregulated. America needs to lead the world to create an international framework for monitoring climate change, researching geoengineering options, and regulating the use of geoengineering to make sure it is never deployed without global agreement and only when meeting the highest requirements for safety.

4. **Climate Disaster Relief** – Each country would commit to helping developing countries that are ravaged by climate disasters for humanitarian reasons and to promote stability. Just like America used the Marshall Plan to stabilize Western Europe after World War II, we should provide more technical and humanitarian assistance to countries facing climate disasters out of our own national self-interests.

When we have formed an alliance among the large greenhouse gas producing countries, we should then reach out to other countries to invite their participation. America should lead the world away from the brink of climate disaster into a new global alliance for sustainability.

We should use our position as the world's economic leader to show that climate action is good for business and the economy. We should use our position as the world's technological leader to deploy technologies to slash greenhouse gas emissions. We should use our position as the world's humanitarian leader to foster goodwill, friendship, and stability. We should use our position as the world's social and cultural leader to support a new global ethic for conservation and sustainability.

Building a Climate Movement

Americans are ready to make the fight against climate change our new national purpose. Business leaders, faith leaders, military leaders, and ordinary citizens are looking to support strong national political leaders committed to climate action. I am hopeful our current national political leaders are up to the task. We can help them by speaking up and building a movement for climate action. If our movement is strong, our national political leaders will either embrace climate action along with us, or we will replace them.

Americans need to speak up with their elected officials and candidates about climate change. In Iowa, we have a unique opportunity, and responsibility, to talk to presidential candidates who are visiting our state for the first-in-the-nation precinct caucuses about the issue. So, too, do the citizens of New Hampshire, South Carolina, Nevada, and other early primary and caucus states. Over the years, I have talked to Vice President Gore, then-Governor George W. Bush, then-Senator Clinton, and President Obama about climate change. I know others in Iowa who talked to Mitt Romney, Newt Gingrich, Ron Paul, and Rick Santorum before the 2012 caucuses. We need more people to speak up in support of national climate action.

We also need more people to write, call, and visit our Congressional representatives and Senators. In 2013,

I helped organize an event called "Climate Action Across Iowa" in which hundreds of Iowans visited 21 Congressional and Senate offices in ten cities across our state on a single day to support climate action. If you do not tell your elected officials and candidates that you want climate action, how will they know? Your actions can be the beginning of strong American leadership on climate change. Now is the time for climate action.

Here is my eight-point action plan for citizens to convince our political leaders to make the fight against climate change our new national purpose:

1. **Get Involved** – Join or organize a local group in your community that meets at least monthly for climate education and advocacy. Many groups such as the Sierra Club, 350.org, Citizens Climate Lobby, Interfaith Power & Light, or the National Wildlife Federation can help you get started. You need to get involved to make a difference.

2. **Get Connected** – Get on the email lists for national advocacy groups like those mentioned above or other national groups like the Natural Resources Defense Council, the Union of Concerned Scientists, and the Environmental Defense Fund, and use social media to connect locally and around the world for climate action.

3. **Talk to Congress** – Write and call your Congressional representative and Senators to tell them you support climate action. Contact them at either their local in-district offices or their Washington, D.C., office. Ask your friends to do the same. Hold parties to write letters and postcards to them asking for climate action. Meet in person with your Congressional representative and Senators or their staff. You do not need a big group. Even one person can ask for a meeting.

4. **Write Letters to the Editor** – Letters to the editor and guest columns are important because elected of-

ficials read them and because they help educate the public. When writing a letter to the editor or a guest column, try to find a news hook, like recent news coverage about global warming or climate disasters, then call for climate action.

5. **Publicize Your Efforts** – Alert the local news media (newspapers, radio and television stations, bloggers) about your advocacy and education efforts, especially when you are advocating for climate legislation or holding educational events for the public.

6. **Reach Out To Community Groups** – Educate other community groups (business, civic, and faith organizations) about climate change and ask them to support climate action with your Congressional representative and Senators. We need more business leaders, civic leaders, and faith leaders to speak up for climate action.

7. **Raise Money** – Use some of the money you save by conserving energy to support climate advocacy groups, as well as disaster relief organizations like the American Red Cross.

8. **Run for Office** – If your Congressional representative and Senators do not support climate action, you can run for office and you can win.

By getting involved, you can make a difference. A group of committed citizens in every Congressional district in America can make a difference. After the heat and drought of 2012, after Hurricane Sandy, and after all of the other climate disasters of recent years, Americans are ready for climate action. Together, we can grow a movement for the climate action we so urgently need for sustainability, health, and prosperity in the climate century and beyond.

Your Personal Climate Action
To-Do List:

These are the actions I will take in my personal life: (See pp. 69-87 for some ideas.)

1. _____

2. _____

3. _____

4. _____

5. _____

These are the actions I will take to promote public policy: (See pp. 110-112 for specific actions you can take.)

1. _____

2. _____

3. _____

4. _____

5. _____

Appendix
Responding to Doubting Thomas

I first prepared "Responding to Doubting Thomas" when I worked for Ecumenical Ministries of Iowa in 1999. Over the years, the claims of skeptics have grown weaker, as the scientific understanding of climate change has improved. Still, some Americans continue to doubt the reality of climate change. Here are 18 arguments skeptics make against climate action and my responses to them. When you hear people assert the arguments of the skeptics, feel free to use this as a reference on possible ways to respond.

1. Global warming is "junk science." Skeptics say that global warming is based on "junk science." The best way to respond to this type of comment is to find out what part of the climate science the skeptic thinks is junk. Does the person disagree with the natural greenhouse effect, the buildup of greenhouse gases, the warming of the earth, or the causal connection between greenhouse gases and warming? Once a specific concern is identified, it is easier to discuss. If the skeptic does not have any specific concern, just say that few if any issues have been more thoroughly studied and, unfortunately, the consensus is that it is real, it is caused primarily by humans, and it poses real dangers for America, so we have to deal with it. Ignoring it will not make it go away.

2. Carbon dioxide is plant food, not a pollutant. Skeptics say that carbon dioxide cannot be bad for us because it helps plants grow. This argument is not valid. No one is advocating for the elimination of all atmospheric carbon dioxide (even if humans had the ability to do that). What we want to stop is the addition of carbon dioxide to the atmosphere that is making the oceans more acidic, is favoring some plant species over others, has a global heating effect, and is changing the climate in dangerous ways.

3. Humans only account for a small fraction of carbon dioxide. Skeptics say that humans produce little carbon dioxide compared to natural sources such as volcanoes or decay of organic matter. That is true, but what it overlooks is that nature absorbs the carbon dioxide produced from natural sources. The human addition of carbon dioxide has knocked the carbon cycle out of balance and is causing the steady buildup of carbon dioxide in the atmosphere. As for volcanic eruptions, they have a short-term cooling effect due to the sulfate aerosols they produce. Although volcanoes can add greenhouse gases to the atmosphere over long geological time periods, they are not the cause of the rapid and ongoing increase in carbon dioxide in the atmosphere over the last two centuries. Humans are.

4. Water vapor is the primary greenhouse gas. Skeptics point out, correctly, that water vapor is the primary greenhouse gas. What it overlooks is that carbon dioxide is also a greenhouse gas that is causing global warming. It also overlooks the scientific understanding that as humans add carbon dioxide and other greenhouse gases to the atmosphere, the warming they cause will likely lead to even more water vapor in the atmosphere, magnifying the warming.

5. Scientists warned us about an ice age in the 1970s. Skeptics say that the earth was cooling in the 1970s and that scientists then projected that the earth would be entering a new ice age. They argue that if scientists were wrong then, why should be believe them now? That argument is not valid for three basic reasons.

First, the isolated projections of a coming ice age by a few scientists in the 1970s is not equivalent to today's thorough scientific understanding of global warming and climate change.

Second, if not for greenhouse gases, the earth might slowly be entering a new ice age. Small amounts of greenhouse gases from human activity might be valuable to prevent global cooling, but that does not mean we should now produce so many greenhouse gases that we heat the planet and cause dangerous climatic changes.

Third, the record does show that the Northern Hemisphere did cool slightly from 1940 to 1970. Scientists now understand that this was caused largely by the short-term cooling influence of sulfate aerosols produced by heavy industrial pollution in the Northern Hemisphere during that time. The cooling effect of sulfate aerosols is short-term, however, and sulfur emissions have been controlled since 1970 through the Clean Air Act and technological improvements, unmasking the longer-term global warming influence of greenhouse gases. The scientific understanding of sulfate aerosols was confirmed in 1991 when Mt. Pinatubo erupted, producing significant sulfate aerosols around the world. As projected, there was a short-term global cooling that lasted approximately 18 months from the sulfate aerosols from Mt. Pinatubo.

6. It is not warming; we still have cold, snowy days. Skeptics argue that the earth cannot be warming because we still have days with cold temperatures and considerable snow and ice. This argument is not valid. We will still have cold days, especially during the early decades of climate change. Overall, however, the earth is warming and changing the climate in dangerous ways. Record snows and ice may actually result from global warming, as warming adds moisture to the atmosphere and changes weather and precipitation patterns. In fact, because of climate change, we should expect more extreme winter precipitation events.

7. It is the urban heat island effect, not global warming. Skeptics sometimes blame the "urban heat island effect" for the perception of global warming. The urban heat island effect occurs when urbanization warms a locality. The modern temperature records that are used to calculate global average warming, however, do not include data influenced by the urban heat island effect. Moreover, the urban heat island effect cannot explain phenomena like increasing global ocean temperatures or the loss of Arctic sea ice.

8. It is solar variation. Skeptics often blame "solar variation" for global warming, sometimes asserting that Mars is warming, too. The fact is that solar variation has been measured and found to contribute only a small fraction of the warming measured to date (+0.12 watts per square meter), much less than the role of greenhouse gases from human activity (+2.64 watts per square meter).

9. Global warming is just natural; we are not causing it. Skeptics claim that global warming is natural, suggesting that humans are not causing it. This argument is not valid because possible natural causes have been thoroughly assessed and measured and they cannot account for the warming that has been measured to date. The human production of greenhouse gases is now the primary driver of global warming and climate change. It is true that climate has changed in the past for natural reasons, but the fact that climate can change for natural reasons does not mean that human activity cannot trigger climate change.

10. Clouds will prevent global warming. Skeptics suggest that clouds will stop global warming. Some cloud formations warm the earth; others have a cooling effect. Overall, clouds have been assessed and so far have been found to have a cooling effect (-0.70 watts per square meter) that has offset some of the global warming from greenhouse gases. The cooling effect of clouds, however, is far less than the warming effect of greenhouse gases (+2.64 watts per square meter). Hoping that clouds will somehow offset enough global warming in the future is not a responsible policy response to the accelerating buildup of carbon dioxide and other greenhouse gases in the atmosphere.

11. Global warming is natural so we should just live with it. Skeptics argue that the earth has had warm periods (and ice ages) without any interference by humans before, so if humans warm the earth now, what's the problem? Newt Gingrich made this argument at a forum on Energy and the Presidency I attended in November 2011, by saying to a questioner who asked him about global warming, "Let me ask you, what is the right temperature for the planet?" The answer to former Speaker Gingrich's question is simple: The right temperature for the earth is the relatively stable average temperature that has allowed human population to grow from a few million to seven billion today. Climate change today will cause significant hardship for people and property adapted to past climate conditions. Although climate has changed in the ancient past, it has never changed this much, this fast, in a world with so many people.

12. Global warming will be good for us. Skeptics sometimes argue that global warming will be good for us, citing longer growing seasons in places like Greenland and Canada. Those places, however, do not have adequate soils to support high levels of production. Moreover, whatever "benefits" global warming may bring, they will be overwhelmed by the huge costs from ocean acidification, sea level rise, changes in weather and precipitation, changes in the ranges of plants, insects, and animals, climate-related disasters, and the other consequences of climate change.

13. We can just adapt to global warming. Some skeptics say we should just wait for climate change then adapt to it. At this point, however, we will already have to adapt regardless of what we do. Adaptation will be costly and difficult. Given the momentum in the climate system, it is unclear to which climate system people should try to adapt. It will become even more costly as the earth continues to warm and the climate continues to change. Instead of waiting, we need to reduce greenhouse gases as soon as possible to minimize climate change, at the same time that we invest heavily in new infrastructure and other measures to make us more resilient in the face of climatic changes that can no longer be avoided.

14. Disasters have always occurred, so how is global warming different? Skeptics point out, correctly, that disasters have always happened in the past. Where they are mistaken is the implication that we therefore do not need to worry about global warming. Global warming is causing more frequent and severe disasters, like a baseball player who hits more home runs using steroids. Regardless of the cause of disasters, however, we need to invest in more pre-disaster hazard mitigation. By making such investments, we can safeguard our people and our property in the face of future climate disasters, as well as future disasters that would have happened naturally.

15. The policies to fight climate change are worse than climate change. Skeptics increasingly argue that climate change may be a real problem, but the solutions are all worse than climate change. They believe we are so dependent on fossil fuels that reducing our use of them will wreck our economy and make poverty even worse. This is wrong because investing in clean energy and transportation solutions will actually create jobs, support businesses, improve health, and save energy costs. Morever, we can shape policies to account for the need to reduce poverty and adjust policies as needed in the future. By contrast, ignoring climate change will *irreversibly* commit us to more warming and climate change in the future. This would hurt the poor and create a drag on our economy, as we suffer even higher health costs and disaster costs in the future. Ultimately, more frequent and severe climate disasters would ruin our economy.

16. America cannot act because China and India will not. Skeptics argue that America cannot do anything about climate change without China and India. The fact that China and India want to grow their economies, however, makes the need for climate action more urgent, not less. Each day we delay takes the world to higher levels of greenhouse gases that will produce more climate change and more climate disasters. Instead of delay, Americans need to slash our own greenhouse gas emissions and lead the rest of the world (including China and India) to slash their greenhouse gas emissions, at the same time that we all prepare for the climate change that is now unavoidable. Climate change should take its place at the center of American foreign policy out of our own national self-interests. Not acting because of China and India is a dangerous game of climate chicken.

17. Proposed policies will not be effective in stopping global warming. Skeptics argue that some proposed policies are too weak to actually stop global warming. It is true that some of them are too weak. That is why we need comprehensive climate legislation to slash greenhouse gas emissions, understanding that we also need to prepare for the climatic change that cannot be avoided. Regardless, everything we do to reduce greenhouse gases will slow down climate change and buy time for more dramatic reductions later. By contrast, doing nothing commits us to ever increasing warming and disasters in the future.

18. The policies to fight climate change will take away our freedom. Skeptics argue that in a free society, climate change is just a price we have to pay for freedom. America has never provided a right to pollute, however. Nuisance laws restrict what one property owner can do to the air or water of his or her neighbors. Moreover, we can shape our policies to protect and promote Americans' freedom of choice. By contrast, ignoring climate change will threaten our freedom. During climate disasters, people lose their freedoms, and as those disasters grow more frequent and severe because of climate change, Americans will have less freedom. To ensure freedom in the climate century, we need climate action now.

> Remember:
> a Doubting Thomas
> today can be a leader
> for climate action
> tomorrow.